WE ARE POWER

How Nonviolent Activism CHANGES THE WORLD

TODD HASAK-LOWY

ABRAMS BOOKS FOR YOUNG READERS · NEW YORK

Cataloging-in-Publication Data has been applied for and may be obtained from the Library of Congress.

Paperback ISBN 978-1-4197-6010-5

Edited by Howard W. Reeves
Book design by Charice Silverman

Published in paperback in 2022 by Abrams Books for Young Readers, an imprint of ABRAMS. Originally published in hardcover by Abrams Books for Young Readers in 2020.

Printed and bound in U.S.A.
10 9 8 7 6 5 4 3 2 1

ABRAMS The Art of Books
195 Broadway, New York, NY 10007
abramsbooks.com

To the next generation of nonviolent activists,

CONTENTS

Introduction

Rethinking History: Who Makes It? And How?

WHEN WE THINK ABOUT THE HISTORY OF THE UNITED States since the start of the twentieth century, a range of events come to mind:

- World War I
- The Great Depression
- World War II
- The Korean War
- The Vietnam War
- The assassination of John F. Kennedy
- The assassination of Martin Luther King Jr.
- The moon landing
- The invention of the Internet
- 9/11
- The War in Afghanistan
- The Iraq War

Conventional Power. American soldiers battle Iraqi insurgents in 2004.

What does this list tell us? Well, almost half of it is wars, which maybe shouldn't come as a surprise. We're often taught that history revolves around wars, because wars decisively change the path of history. In a war, power belongs to the politicians who declare war, and to the generals who wage the battles.

In the twentieth century alone, 187 million people died in wars around the world as armies clashed again and again.

But what about the other events here? A couple relate to technology and innovation. Almost all of the rest involve civilians claiming power for themselves, and doing so violently, by taking the lives of others, through assassinations or terrorism.

Does that mean history is mostly violence?

If the answer is yes, then are you powerless to shape the future if you're not a politician or a general or someone willing to take someone else's life?

Here are two other major events from the same time period: the ratification of the Nineteenth Amendment—granting women suffrage, the right to vote—in 1920, and the passage of the Civil Rights Act—outlawing racial segregation—in 1964. These events changed millions of lives. One finally gave half the population a voice; the other ended decades of legal, institutionalized racism.

History is more than wars and violence.

In fact, history has often been forged through conflicts of a different sort, when huge numbers of people banded together to fight and sacrifice for their side, without ever joining a conventional army or resorting to violence. Incredible individuals—who were not politicians or generals—led these movements.

In the case of the Nineteenth Amendment, the people who fought were mostly women. They had almost no official voice in the political process, and no armed soldiers on their side. But eventually, these women overpowered—and eventually persuaded—an American president and a majority of the country's male elected officials to back their cause.

The people who fought for the Civil Rights Act were mostly African Americans. Discriminated against and marginalized by the very racism they opposed, these men and women were regularly denied the vote. Often, they were violently attacked. But in the end, they convinced great numbers of white Americans (and the white politicians who represented them) to reject the racism that once ruled their lives.

In both conflicts, one side was excluded from governance and had no conventional weapons, yet this side prevailed each time, and without shedding their opponents' blood.

So what was the source of their remarkable power? *Nonviolent activism.*

Alice Paul led the final push for the Nineteenth Amendment. She was a Quaker woman with no access to the voting booth. Martin Luther King Jr. led the call for the Civil Rights Act. He was a Baptist minister who held no public office and couldn't drink from the same water fountains as whites.

Both Paul and King were activists who inspired,

mobilized, and organized vast numbers of people to unite in order to struggle and sacrifice together for their causes. Operating outside of government institutions and rejecting violent methods, women's suffrage and the civil rights movement used nonviolent resistance to transform their people's weakness into strength and change the course of history.

Nonviolent activism isn't just an American phenomenon. Perhaps the greatest nonviolent struggle of all, the Indian independence movement, led by Mohandas K. Gandhi, ended nearly two hundred years of British colonial rule and brought freedom to 300 million people without a bloody war of independence. Nonviolent struggles also helped overthrow totalitarian regimes shaped by the Soviet Union, one of the largest, most powerful, and most repressive countries ever.

Many times in the past, nonviolent resistance has prevailed, shifting the course of history as much as a war—without firing a single shot.

So maybe we've been getting our history wrong.

Or at least very incomplete.

But what exactly *is* nonviolent activism? Is *any* activism that rejects violence automatically considered non violent activism?

No.

Nonviolent activists employ disruptive, risky tactics that challenge those in power and interrupt the way things normally work—without taking up arms.

As we'll see in the chapters that follow, nonviolent activists can call on all sorts of techniques and tactics to advance their cause. Gene Sharp, a scholar of nonviolent activism, put together a list of all the methods that have been used in nonviolent struggles around the world.

How many entries made his list?

One hundred and ninety-eight!

Protests, strikes, boycotts, and intentional law-breaking—what's called civil disobedience—are just some of the best-known methods nonviolent activists can use. But whatever techniques they eventually choose, their successful application first requires the organization and mobilization of large groups of people willing to challenge the powers that be.

Quite often, the initial stages of organization require activism that, while peaceful, isn't technically *nonviolent* activism. Why? Because this organization takes place within institutions and systems that are entirely legal and permitted by the government.

For instance, women won the right to vote in the

Nonviolent Power. Student protesters take to the streets to demand stronger gun control in Boston on March 24, 2018.

United States in 1920, but their movement, the suffrage movement, actually started way back in 1848. For many decades, suffragists held meetings, gave speeches, circulated petitions, wrote editorials, lobbied politicians, and even went to court to argue that the law already gave them the right to vote.

This *institutional* activism raised awareness, shifted public opinion, brought thousands and thousands of people into the movement, and even won some victories (such as when individual states amended their constitutions to give women the vote). But as vital as these methods were, they weren't truly the stuff of nonviolent activism. It was only after sixty-plus years of playing by the rules in order to change these rules that some suffragists decided it was time for a more radical approach. It was time to bend and even break the rules. That's when nonviolent activism entered the movement, in the form of sustained protest, civil disobedience, and hunger strikes.

In most of the stories you'll read in this book, institutional activism forms the backdrop of the conflicts and movements in question. Gandhi was an activist lawyer before becoming a nonviolent activist willing to break the law. The disruptive Montgomery Bus Boycott was inspired in part by court victories declaring segregation unconstitutional. And before leading the farmworkers' strike and grape boycott, Cesar Chavez set about organizing farmworkers into a union.

Institutional activism is crucial to fighting for justice, and there are plenty of great books about that kind of activism. But this book focuses on those times when such activism isn't enough, when injustice is so stubborn that more drastic action is needed.

So that's what nonviolent activism *is*. But how does it work? In an age when armies are stronger than ever before, when guns seem to be everywhere, how can people defeat their adversaries without resorting to violence themselves?

The best way to answer these questions is by telling the stories of some of the most incredible, inspiring nonviolent struggles of the last one hundred years. Which isn't to say that nonviolent resistance is a new phenomenon. Not at all. In fact, its history goes back many centuries and includes even the biblical Jesus among its innumerable practitioners. But this simple method of pursuing justice has seen a remarkable resurgence over the last century. And as we'll see, though these movements have much in common, each conflict is unique and teaches us something new about how and why nonviolent action works.

Yet all these stories do have one thing in common: nonviolent activists who have chosen to *fight* against injustice and the people behind it. You might think that someone who practices nonviolence must hate conflict, but the exact opposite is true. Nonviolent activists are fighters who directly challenge their opponents; only the wars they wage look a lot different than the ones that take place on a military battlefield.

I wrote this book because I believe that nonviolence—even more effective than it is peaceful—is a better way to fight. Indeed, it may well be the best way to fix our broken world.

I hope after reading these pages you'll agree, and be inspired to join those already fighting for change, nonviolently.

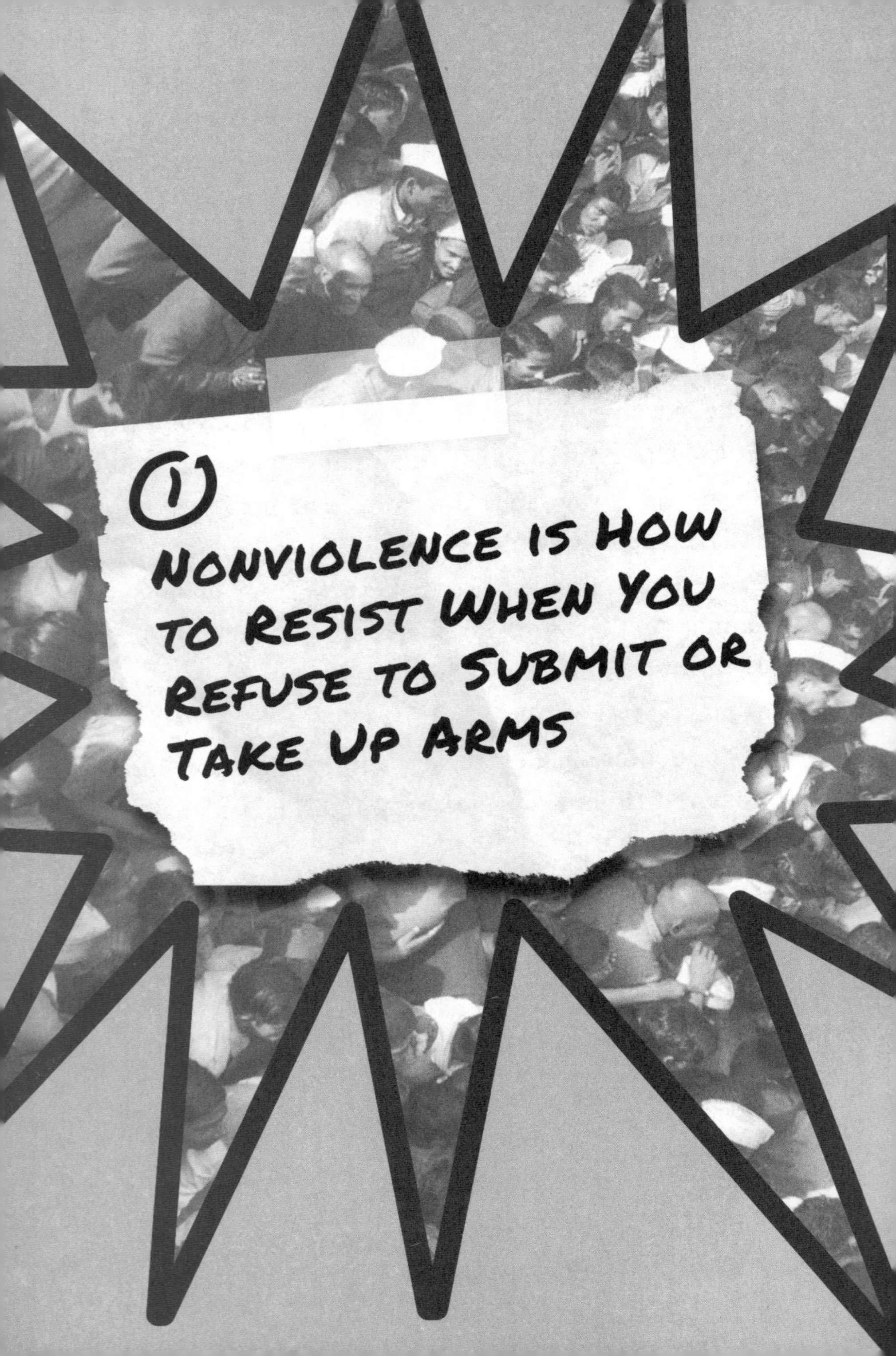

1 Nonviolence Is How to Resist When You Refuse to Submit or Take Up Arms

GANDHI and INDIAN INDEPENDENCE

Mohandas K. Gandhi, leader of the Indian Independence movement, in 1942

"I regard myself as a soldier, though a soldier of peace."

—GANDHI

ON SEPTEMBER 11, 1906, MOHANDAS KARAMCHAND Gandhi, a lawyer and leader of the Indian community in South Africa, then part of the British Empire, took the stage in Johannesburg's Empire Theatre for the second time that day. As he looked out into the half-lit theater, illuminated only by the bright rays of sunlight coming through its windows, he saw not a single empty seat. Men filled the floor, the galleries, the balconies, and claimed all the standing room as well. The capacity of the theater was around two thousand, but closer to three thousand Indians were now packed inside. Indeed, behind Gandhi the stage held another two hundred chairs.

The angry, agitated crowd had gathered here to protest the Asiatic Law Amendment Ordinance, what they called the Black Act, which demanded that every Indian in the Transvaal Colony register with the government. Transvaal was one of a handful of British colonies in South Africa, where some 150,000 Indian workers and their families lived. According to the new ordinance, Indians in Transvaal would have their fingerprints taken, while identifying marks on their bodies would be recorded, despite the fact that such steps were traditionally reserved for criminals only. All Indians would be required to carry this registration certificate with them and could be asked to produce it any time, any place. Failure to comply with the ordinance might lead to arrest, prison, and perhaps even expulsion from the colony.

In a later memoir, Gandhi would recall his first humiliating encounter with the proposed ordinance:

> I shuddered as I read the sections . . . one after another. I saw nothing in it except hatred of Indians. It seemed to me that if the Ordinance was passed and the Indians meekly accepted it, that would spell absolute ruin for the Indians in South Africa . . . Better die than submit to such a law. But how were we to die? What should we dare and do so that there would be nothing before us except a choice of victory or death? An impenetrable wall was before me . . . and I could not see my way through it.

Those crowded inside the Empire Theatre were determined to resist. But how? What power did they have?

At the opening of the September 11 meeting, Gandhi had explained the details of the Ordinance to those in attendance. The organizers had planned to next present and pass a number of resolutions declaring their rejection of the Black Act. But the speakers following Gandhi had whipped the angry crowd into a frenzy, calling on them not merely to refuse registering and thus prepare themselves for the possibility of jail, but to take a solemn oath in order to cement their opposition.

Gandhi, though not scheduled to speak again, asked for permission to address the crowd once more, because he wanted his fellow countrymen to understand the full magnitude of taking a solemn oath. He was perhaps now seeing a way for all of them to pass together through that impenetrable wall, but it wouldn't be easy. The raucous crowd fell silent as the London-trained lawyer, dressed in suit and tie, spoke:

> We may have to go to jail . . . We may be flogged . . . We may be deported. Suffering from starvation and similar hardships in jail, some of

us may fall ill and even die . . . We shall have to suffer all that and worse. If some one asks me when and how the struggle may end, I may say that if the entire community manfully stands the test, the end will be near . . . If I am warning you of the risks attendant upon the pledge, I am at the same time inviting you to pledge yourselves, and I am fully conscious of my responsibility in the matter . . . There is only one course open to some one like me, to die but not to submit to the law.

The Indian community in South Africa already held Mr. Gandhi in high esteem. For more than a decade he had advocated for them diligently, using any and all legal means to fight for them in the face of constant discrimination. Gandhi was already an activist combating injustice, but his weapon was colonial law, his field of battle the courts. He had fought this way because he believed his people could prove their worth as obedient, honorable subjects of the British Empire. This is why he studied law in London and why he dressed like his Western rulers.

But on September 11, 1906, Gandhi's approach to his people's struggle took a radical turn. He now saw that the laws themselves were the problem, because the white South Africans writing them viewed his people as unworthy of basic respect and equal rights. Cooperation suddenly seemed foolish, a surefire way to sabotage their collective future. Hence the lawyer's advice to his community: Commit to civil disobedience. That is, intentionally break this unjust law as a form of protest against it.

To prove his conviction, he pledged to join them, even if it cost him his life.

Thousands of hands shot up in the air and the oath was taken. The crowd cheered in celebration, transforming Gandhi into a new kind of leader. The lawyer was casting off his old tools in order to fashion new ones: the tools of nonviolent resistance.

No two stories of nonviolent struggle are the same. Nevertheless, many of them share a few common features.

When oppressed by a stronger power—an immoral government, an invading force, a greedy boss—it might seem like the weaker party only has two choices.

The first: Submit. Give in, simply do what your oppressor wants, or more accurately, demands. Play by the unfair rules your oppressor put in place.

The second: Take up arms and fight back violently.

Neither of these are terribly appealing. If we give in, we accept our weakness and the oppression that comes with it. We play a game designed with our defeat in mind. But if we fight back violently, we're still likely to lose, otherwise we wouldn't call our opponent the stronger power to begin with. And this loss is almost certain to come at a terribly painful cost, because once you resort to violence you give your powerful adversary permission to do the same.

This bind, this choice between two uninviting strategies, was the source of the "impenetrable wall" that Gandhi confronted with such dismay when he first read the Black Act. But then he discovered, quite spontaneously, a third way.

The third way is nonviolent resistance.

The third way rejects violence without accepting submission. Even more important, it rejects the idea that the oppressed lack power. The third way embraces the need for conflict and the belief that the coming battle can be won. The third way looks out from the stage of the Empire Theatre, sees three thousand "weak" men united in their oath not to obey and their readiness to sacrifice their freedom instead, and realizes that together they possess enormous power.

•

The oath to choose jail over registering was spontaneous, and soon Gandhi was trying to decide how to refer to what they had all vowed to do. The name he first used, one he hadn't invented, was the English phrase "passive resistance." But Gandhi disliked this term, for at least three reasons. First, "passive" was all wrong. There was nothing passive about *acting* against an unjust government, even if this action wasn't violent. After all, by mid-November of 1907, four months after the ordinance went into effect, Indians in South Africa were standing trial and going to jail. Intentionally, and actively.

Second, Gandhi preferred a term from an Indian language, since it was important to him that everyone in this struggle "respect our own language, speak it well and use in it as few foreign words as possible." This was a showdown between Indians and white South Africans, in which the Indians sought to demonstrate that they were equals. If they needed someone else's language to do this, what chance did they have?

Third, Gandhi believed that even a passive resister could resist out of hatred, could resist while experiencing internal violence. Gandhi, growing more religious throughout this period and seeing this new path as not just a political strategy but as an entire way of life, needed a different name for their strategy, a name expressing the positive features of this resistance. Lacking any great ideas himself, he placed a contest in *Indian Opinion*, the newspaper he had begun publishing in 1903. The contest was announced in the last issue of 1907, which was printed the very day that Gandhi himself was tried and convicted for failing to register. The winner would get ten copies of a pamphlet on the Black Act.

In early January a winner was chosen, though the winning entry required some modification. The final term settled on was "satyagraha." "Satya" is Sanskrit for truth, while "agraha" means holding firmly. Sometimes the term is translated as "truth force" or "soul force." Noting the close ties between truth and love, Gandhi once said satyagraha is the force "born of Truth and Love or nonviolence."

Activist Lawyer. For most of his years in South Africa, Gandhi dressed like the British-trained lawyer he was.

The rest of Gandhi's life would be devoted to satyagraha, to discovering how it might be used, to learning just how strong it could be. Indeed, he called his autobiography *The Story of My Experiments with the Truth*.

On January 10, 1908, Gandhi appeared before a judge, because he had failed to leave the Transvaal Colony within forty-eight hours, as he was ordered to do near the end of 1907 for refusing to register. Many other Indians had already been arrested and tried, since only about one in ten Indians had registered so far. Gandhi represented dozens of them in court. Now it was his turn to stand as the defendant.

Gandhi pleaded guilty and made a highly unusual request: he wanted the "heaviest penalty" under the law.

Why would a man, already in trouble, be asking for even more trouble?

Gandhi was still learning how to sharpen "the sword of satyagraha." Combining Western sources, like Jesus's instruction in the Sermon on the Mount to "turn the other cheek," with the sacred concept of *ahimsa* (love or noninjury) as understood by the Jain religion in India, Gandhi crafted both a new philosophy and a radical method for creating change as well. By 1908 he already understood a basic principle of nonviolent resistance. "Our whole struggle is based on our submitting ourselves to hardships, not inflicting them on anyone else." Satyagraha seeks out conflict, and conflict often means suffering. But in a nonviolent campaign the resister—or *satyagrahi*, as Gandhi called him—avoids hurting his adversary. The oppressor is thus given no convenient excuse to retaliate violently. Even better, the resister, by showing his willingness to suffer, demonstrates that no punishment will lead to his surrender. The satyagrahi shows his strength through his ability to endure hardship.

By asking for the most severe sentence, Gandhi proved to the authorities he did not fear them. Not their threat of punishment, and not even the punishments themselves.

Gandhi requested six months in prison with hard labor, along with a fine of five hundred pounds. But the judge only gave him two months, and no hard labor.

Still, off to prison he went.

Gandhi now sat in the Johannesburg jail.

His freedom had been taken from him, but Gandhi was far from powerless. First of all, he was not alone. Day after day fellow satyagrahis joined him in prison, until tents needed to be set up in the yard to house everyone. And beyond the walls the movement was swelling, determined to show its force. Indians closed their stores in protest of Gandhi's arrest, while the entire conflict spilled over into the neighboring South African colony of Natal, where even more Indian immigrants lived. The power of this movement was in its numbers, and its numbers were increasing each day.

The white leadership in Transvaal was taking notice, including the head of the colony, Jan Christian Smuts, who was alarmed that the threat of jail was having no effect. As he put it, he had "sent every leader to prison, and hundreds more, and it had had no impression." If thousands more Indians acted on their pledge to follow their leaders to jail, there would be no place to put them. The system would break down.

Before the end of January, Gandhi was taken from jail by police escort to meet with Smuts in Pretoria, the capital of Transvaal.

The two men negotiated a possible settlement. They agreed to these basic terms: Indians would register voluntarily, prisoners would be released, and there would be future talks about repealing the Asiatic Act altogether. Smuts then asked Gandhi that the Indians "not crow over their victory," that they, in other words, not celebrate publicly.

Gandhi agreed.

This exchange with Smuts, including Gandhi's promise that his side not gloat, tells us a great deal about how nonviolent activists understand the proper way to resolve a conflict. Even after he was brought to Pretoria, thanks to the strength his movement had demonstrated, Gandhi's goal wasn't simply to get everything he could for his side. It wasn't as if any Indian wanted to register, even voluntarily, but registering this way was definitely an improvement over a law that forced one to.

Gandhi's goal was compromise, not one-sided victory.

But why compromise, why settle for less than everything you want if your power is only growing day by day? Because even though no one completely wins in a compromise, no one loses, either. Gandhi understood that he and his people were in the middle of a fight with a sometimes cruel and often arrogant opponent, but he also hoped that in the end the two sides would continue living side by side. That being the case, there was little value in resoundingly beating and humiliating Smuts.

Gandhi's belief in making sure no one loses also explains the promise that his people not gloat, despite the fact that they had plenty to gloat about. They had stood up to an unfair racist law, accepted jail rather than obey, and this courageous strategy had paid off. It would only be natural, especially for a mass movement like this one, to take to the streets to celebrate the fact that their imprisoned leader had successfully negotiated with the head of the colony on nearly equal footing.

But Gandhi sought a greater victory: true reconciliation. The aim of satyagraha wasn't merely to defeat the other side without injuring them; it was to change their relationship altogether. The opponent of the Indian nonviolent movement was injustice itself, not white South Africans. Victory would only be won when everyone enjoyed equal rights and everyone's dignity was respected.

But even after his successful negotiations with Smuts, such a victory remained elusive.

The compromise Gandhi and Smuts struck hinged on their agreement that at some future date there would be talks about getting rid of the Asiatic Act once and for all. But this wouldn't happen, at least not in the short term.

Though these two very different men managed to see nearly eye to eye, their compromise had plenty of detractors among both whites and Indians. On their way to register voluntarily in Johannesburg on February 10, 1908, Gandhi and a couple associates were assaulted by some of their own countrymen, who angrily opposed registration of any kind. Gandhi was struck on the back of his head with a stick or an iron rod and knocked to the ground, where he was beaten unconscious. Luckily one of his friends, Thambi Naidoo, was carrying an umbrella that he used to fend off the assailants. Still, Gandhi would require six stitches.

Meanwhile, Smuts—under pressure from his people and perhaps regretting the terms of the compromise—sought to end the period of voluntary registration after three months, at which time the Black Act would go back into effect. He and Gandhi met repeatedly in June, but no new compromise could be reached. Gandhi, recognizing that "in any great war, more than one battle has to be fought," prepared for a new round of satyagraha.

At 4:00 p.m. on Sunday, August 16, three thousand Asians—Indians as well as Chinese, who were also subject to the Asiatic Act—gathered outside the Fordsburg Mosque in Johannesburg. It should be noted that Native Africans, in the middle of their own struggle against the British, were not included in the movement Gandhi was leading. In fact, early on in his time in South Africa, Gandhi often referred to them using the derogatory term "Kaffir." He gradually began to view them differently and came to see the common elements in their struggles, but Gandhi would leave South Africa without ever seeking to unite their causes.

On this August day a four-legged iron cauldron had been set up. Two thousand registration certificates, collected beforehand, were dumped into the pot. Next they were soaked with paraffin—a waxy, flammable liquid—and then set on fire.

A local newspaper describes what happened next: "The crowd hurrahed and shouted themselves hoarse; hats were thrown in the air, and whistles blown." Many more in attendance, who until the bonfire was lit had second thoughts about burning their own certificates, approached the platform and added theirs to the blaze.

Gandhi was summoned to meet once more with Smuts in Pretoria the very next day. A new compromise was reached: the Asiatic Act would not be repealed, but would rather be treated as a dead letter, a law the authorities would not enforce.

Another victory for Gandhi and his people, perhaps. But all the while South African whites, determined to dominate this society completely, continued passing other discriminatory laws, such as one preventing any Indians, no matter their social standing or education, from entering the Transvaal Colony from other South African colonies, such as Natal and Orange River.

•

And so the conflict continued in this fashion for another five years. New discriminatory laws, protests, imprisonment, and negotiations leading to possible compromises that were then undermined by a new batch of unfair laws.

Though he himself hadn't been to the land of his birth for years, word of Gandhi's leadership and accomplishments was spreading back home in India. And with every day that passed, he became more and more convinced that satyagraha contained within itself boundless power. "A more reliable and more honorable method of fighting injustice than any which has heretofore been adopted," he wrote.

In the spring of 1913 a new, hardline immigration bill was drafted by the South African government that made it clear Indian interests would never truly be honored in this ongoing struggle. Among other things, it seriously restricted the rights of Indians to move from one colony to another. It also failed to repeal a three-pound tax, a significant sum, imposed on Indian workers who chose to remain in South Africa after their labor contracts, which had first brought them to the country, expired. Last, it failed to weigh in on a conflict stemming from yet another recent discriminatory legal decision, according to which traditional Hindi and Muslim marriages would not be recognized.

In response to this bill, a new satyagraha campaign was set in motion. On September 15, sixteen Indians marched to enter Transvaal illegally. Though this method of nonviolent protest had been tried before, this time around some of the satyagrahis were women, something unheard of back then, since in "India itself, the idea that women could participate in popular social movements was out of the question." Gender roles were quite restrictive in Indian society at this time. Middle-class women, for instance, "were not supposed to leave the house unescorted."

But during an earlier trip to London to advocate for his people before members of Parliament and even Lord Elgin, secretary of state for the colonies, Gandhi had crossed paths with the British suffragettes (whom we'll learn about in the next chapter), and greatly admired their own nonviolent campaign aimed at winning the right to vote. A truly mass nonviolent movement, he realized, would require the participation of men *and* women.

On September 23, all sixteen marchers, including Gandhi's wife, Kasturba, were sentenced to three months in prison. Gandhi himself, not among those who marched, published two powerful pieces in *Indian Opinion*, both calling for all Indians—especially the poor, a group he hadn't singled out before—to now join the struggle. It was no longer enough for the wealthier vanguard of the Indian community to lead by example; the time had come to grow the movement. And by focusing on the tax, which was most difficult for the poor to pay, Gandhi was able to mobilize them as well.

The combination of women's participation and his appeal to the poor sent a potent shock wave through the Indian community. Two thousand workers in Natal went on strike. New marches were organized, many more activists were arrested, and soon thousands upon thousands of Indian laborers all over South Africa—in sugar plantations and coal mines, on railways and ships—were going on strike. Farming was interrupted, a main source of energy grew harder to come by, all while key modes of transportation—for moving people and things—became unreliable.

Without the work of Indian laborers the country could not function.

While leading yet another march in November, Gandhi himself was arrested and sent to jail. When he was released in December, he appeared like a new man. The London-trained lawyer had rejected his Western suit and tie for the simple clothes of an indentured servant. Now barefoot, he had shaved most of his head as well.

Inner Swaraj. In order to claim true freedom, Gandhi rejected Western ways and Western clothes as well.

Why?

Gandhi's goal was independence, what he called *swaraj*, a term meaning freedom both external and internal. Swaraj means not just enjoying political rights but also having the ability to control who you are deep inside. And this inner swaraj couldn't be given to anyone; it had to be claimed. Gandhi now believed that Indians could only acquire this inner swaraj by rejecting Western ways. In years to come, he would spin his own cloth, called *khadi*, dressing himself in simple swaths of fabric, rather than wearing imported clothing.

Swaraj was the goal, the end toward which he and his people were struggling, and satyagraha was the means, the way they'd get there. Because, as he wrote, "only fair means can produce fair results."

This latest, most extensive satyagraha campaign led to more negotiations between Smuts and Gandhi. The eventual outcome of their meeting was the Indians' Relief Bill, which was passed in late June 1914. This bill abolished the tax for those who wished to remain in South Africa and recognized Indian marriages. Though the white leadership was nevertheless still marching headlong toward the discriminatory system of apartheid that would rule South Africa until the 1990s, Gandhi was satisfied with the terms of this settlement.

More than this, he was eager to finally return to India, as he felt his work in South Africa was done. After Gandhi departed from South Africa once and for all on July 18, 1914, a relieved Smuts reflected, "The saint has left our shores—I sincerely hope for ever."

Gandhi now saw satyagraha as "perhaps the mightiest instrument on earth." But could it succeed in India itself? After all, it was one thing to mobilize 150,000 immigrants to demand greater rights. But what about leading 300 million colonial subjects, whose country, India, was the "jewel in the crown" of the British Empire? Could satyagraha bring about the ultimate swaraj, a truly independent India?

On the morning of March 12, 1930, Gandhi and seventy-eight of his followers left Ahmedabad, a village in western India, and began walking due south. Gandhi, now dressed only in khadi, which he had spun himself, held a fifty-four-inch bamboo walking staff with an iron tip. The group's destination was the town of Dandi, on the coast of the Arabian Sea, some 240 miles away.

What would they do once they arrived?

Make salt, by extracting it from the natural saltworks that lined this stretch of the Indian coast.

Gandhi had been back in India for fifteen years by now. During this time, he had traveled throughout the vast countryside again and again in an effort to understand his people, who spoke dozens of different languages and followed just as many traditions. He had worked with a host of political leaders, each with a different vision for how to end almost two hundred years of British rule in India.

And he had imported satyagraha to his homeland. Often the outcomes were promising, such as in the Champaran region in 1917, when poor farmers held protests and went on strike in order to win better conditions from the British landlords who controlled their fields. But not every experiment was successful. In 1922, a noncooperation campaign deteriorated into violence as an angry mob trapped twenty-two policemen in their station and then burned it to the ground, killing everyone inside.

Gandhi had spent some of this time in prison and for a number of years retreated from politics altogether, unsure if he could truly lead his nation or if its people even wanted him to. But by 1928 it had become clear that only Gandhi could unite India behind him. His simple dress, his clear moral vision, and his history of successfully challenging white colonial rule made him a singular figure. More established politicians, such as Jawaharlal Nehru, who would eventually become India's first prime minister, aligned themselves with Gandhi and promoted him as a unique leader who could get results both within and beyond the world of conventional politics.

In 1928 an eleven-member committee of prominent Indian leaders drafted the Nehru Committee Report, which rejected British plans to maintain control of India and instead called for "dominion status," a type of independence. Gandhi announced that a civil disobedience campaign would soon begin if the British did not accept the report.

The British rejected its terms.

Gandhi withdrew to his ashram, a religious retreat, in order to contemplate the form the coming satyagraha would take. He greatly feared another outburst of violence, and he knew that any failure, whether from disunity or lack of impact, would spell disaster for the independence movement as a whole. The country waited anxiously for six weeks, during which time Gandhi remained holed up in his small, spartan hut, listening closely for guidance from his "inner voice."

Eventually the answer came to him: salt.

For almost a hundred years, the British held a monopoly on Indian salt. Indians could neither produce nor sell this most basic of staples. The British levied a salt tax as well, which Indians naturally despised, as it made salt in India "four times as expensive as in England." Even so, there were many more pressing features of British rule Gandhi could have chosen to oppose. But as Gandhi wrote, the simple injustice of this tax made it a perfect target:

> Next to air and water, salt is perhaps the greatest necessity of life. It is the only condiment of the poor . . . There is no article like salt outside water by taxing which the State can reach even the starving millions, the sick, the maimed, and the utterly helpless. The tax constitutes therefore the most inhuman poll tax that ingenuity of man can devise.

Gandhi had chosen his target for satyagraha: he would violate the salt laws by making salt himself. But before actually committing civil disobedience, he reached out to his opponent—Lord Baron Irwin, the British viceroy in India and head of the entire colonial enterprise—with a remarkable letter on March 2 that once again showed the incredible combination of determination and kindness marking Gandhi's approach to conflict.

> "Dear friend," Gandhi began. "Before embarking on Civil Disobedience and taking the risk I have dreaded to take all these years, I would fain approach you and find a way out . . . I cannot intentionally hurt anything that lives, much less fellow human beings, even though they may do the greatest wrong to me and mine. Whilst,

therefore, I hold the British rule to be a curse, I do not intend harm to a single Englishman."

Gandhi continued, explaining why he thought British rule was a curse and explaining how it exploited India's poor—partially through the salt tax—in order to create yet more riches for the British. To make this clear to Irwin personally, Gandhi noted that the viceroy's salary was five thousand times greater than the average Indian made in a year. "Such a system," Gandhi wrote, "deserves to be summarily scrapped."

The coming satyagraha campaign was thus intended to dismantle this system. "Nothing but unadulterated nonviolence can check the organized violence of the British Government," Gandhi told Irwin. This nonviolent approach, Gandhi hoped, would also "convert the British people . . . and thus make them see the wrong they have done to India. I do not seek to harm your people. I want to serve them even as I want to serve my own."

In closing, Gandhi again asked for Irwin's cooperation, so that they might find an alternative to civil disobedience. If Irwin could bring about the "removal of these evils" it would "open the way for a real conference between equals."

"But," Gandhi continued, "if you cannot see your way to deal with these evils and my letter makes no appeal to your heart, on the 11th day of this month I shall proceed with such co-workers of the Ashram as I can take to disregard the provisions of Salt laws."

Lord Irwin's private secretary sent a brief note in reply, stating that the viceroy regretted Gandhi's decision to violate the law.

Gandhi and his fellow unarmed satyagrahis—all men, probably because men and women gathering together in public was still rare in India back then—walked approximately ten miles each day, down winding dirt roads that ran between one small village and another. The days were hot, so they marched only during the cooler mornings and evenings. Still, some struggled with this arduous task and fell sick. But the sixty-year-old Gandhi, despite being the oldest marcher and sleeping only four hours a night due to his many responsibilities, looked, as the perplexed viceroy put it, "regrettably hale and hearty."

In each village where they stopped, Gandhi spoke to excited villagers, educating them about nonviolence, and reminding them, as he first wrote back in 1909, that "the English have not taken India; we have given it to them."

He didn't ask the locals for money to support the campaign. Instead, he implored them to recognize the great power they together held and to prepare themselves to commit civil disobedience after he himself soon broke the law.

Gandhi encouraged local officials, without whose assistance the imperial government could not operate, to resign. Approximately three hundred village leaders along the way did just that. They were beginning to understand their crucial place in the answer to a question that had long mystified the people of India: How can a British imperial force of only 100,000 control a population of 300 million? The answer was Indian cooperation, through which India had "given" their country to the British.

Though they steadily passed from village to village, the procession didn't exactly leave these villages behind. Instead, members of each village joined them, as the number of marchers swelled from just under eighty to several thousand, including many young people and women.

The constant publicity each visit to a village generated propelled the excitement out across India, transforming a winding line of marchers into a nationwide drama. The country, which had already waited weeks for Gandhi to choose the form of the coming satyagraha campaign, now held its breath with anticipation as the marchers steadily neared the coast. Would they march all the way to Dandi or would Gandhi be arrested first? If he reached the shore, would he actually dare to break the law?

The British authorities monitored the march with considerable concern, but they resisted the urge to place Gandhi in jail. For one thing, he had yet to break any law, despite announcing his intention to do so. More than that, the British were well aware that arresting Gandhi would turn him into a martyr for the national cause and further energize an already formidable campaign. As one newspaper wrote: "To arrest Gandhi is to court a war. Not to arrest him is to confess defeat before the war is begun . . . In either case, the Government stands to lose, and Gandhi stands to gain."

The excitement, the attention, and the suspense grew step by step, mile by mile, and day by day. The crowds congregating in the villages and towns along the route to hear Gandhi speak now grew to as many as thirty thousand. Well before they reached the coastal town, the march had become a worldwide story, and Gandhi used the international press to encourage other nations, especially the United States, to side with his people against the British: "I want world sympathy in this battle of Right against Might."

Lawbreaker. Through the simple, defiant act of making salt himself, Gandhi challenged British rule in India.

The procession arrived in Dandi on April 5, the twenty-fourth day of the march. The village's population was normally under five hundred, but now some twelve thousand people were assembled there. At six the next morning, after a sleepless night of prayer, Gandhi entered the sea to purify himself in its waters. A half hour later, standing at the shore, he bent over, scooped up "lumps of natural salt lying in a small pit," and declared, "With this I am shaking the foundations of the British Empire."

The poet Sarojini Naidu, who had traveled to Dandi to witness the event, called out, "Hail, law breaker!"

It was as if Gandhi had challenged his people to join him in an outrageous dare, only to wait twenty-four days before completing his enticing "One . . . two . . ." with a final, delirious "three!" Because just like that, thousands upon thousands of his countrymen, eagerly waiting up and down India's lengthy coastline, began to gather salt water in order to dry it and manufacture salt themselves.

The arrests began.

Members of India's Congress Party were arrested for making salt in pans on the roof of its Bombay headquarters. Jawaharlal Nehru, soon to be arrested himself, described the sudden action of the masses by observing, "It seemed as though a spring had been suddenly released."

Not only did civil disobedience spread, the forms of nonviolent resistance multiplied. In towns and cities far from the coast, boycotts of foreign textiles began. Officials resigned in large numbers. Shops were shuttered and kept closed. Demonstrations were held. People refused to pay taxes. Soon satyagraha was being practiced in every Indian province, with women and the poor and inhabitants of the country's southern regions, all of whom had little if any role in previous campaigns, now taking part. And virtually all of it remained nonviolent, even after Gandhi, one of ninety thousand people to be arrested, was finally taken into custody on May 5.

People Power. Gandhi inspired the Indian masses to claim independence by uniting together behind their overwhelming numbers.

Just like he hoped, nonviolent resistance had united the country against the British. All of India showed that without the consent of the governed, the ruling power has no power at all.

At 2:30 p.m. on February 17, 1931, Gandhi, recently freed from prison, walked up the steps of the viceroy's palace to meet with Lord Irwin. Their subsequent negotiations were, as Gandhi had requested in his letter almost a year earlier, "between equals," a first in the history of British-Indian relations. Lord Irwin represented his nation and Gandhi represented his. Though technically still living in a British colony, Indians were no longer mere

colonial subjects meekly asking their rulers for favors. The civil disobedience campaign, now ten months old, was still underway, and Irwin had come to understand that England could no longer control India without its people's consent.

On March 5, the Gandhi-Irwin Pact was signed and civil disobedience was suspended. Prisoners were freed. The poor were now allowed to manufacture their own salt. But India didn't suddenly claim the independence it sought. Like Gandhi's earlier agreements with Smuts back in South Africa, it was a compromise, and thus an imperfect settlement that was met with plenty of opposition from all sides. But it established that for the first time the Indian political leadership, with Gandhi as its representative, would attend the next Round Table Conference on India's future soon to be held in London.

At last, Indians would now represent India.

There could no longer be any question whether or not India would one day rule itself; the only question was when that inevitable day would come. And unlike so many other colonies around the world, in Asia, Africa, and South America, that already had won or one day would win their freedom only through long, hard, and bloody wars against the colonial forces, India would claim its independence using just a single weapon: the sword of satyagraha.

Gandhi and the people of India had shown, in his words, that "nonviolence is the greatest force at the disposal of mankind. It is mightier than the mightiest weapon of destruction devised by the ingenuity of man."

Gandhi didn't invent nonviolent activism by any means. What he did, however, was reintroduce nonviolent activism to the modern world, popularizing it as a promising, potent alternative to the horrible wars and widescale oppression that had already marred the first half of the twentieth century.

For this reason, many view Gandhi as the father of modern nonviolence, and we'll see his influence in many of the chapters to come. But in our next story, set mostly in the United States, we'll follow a drama that actually took place while Gandhi was still in the thick of his struggle.

The story of these brave activists—suffragists fighting for a woman's right to vote—is often overlooked in the history of nonviolence. But they, too, demonstrated the great promise in waging this kind of fight; they even inspired Gandhi himself.

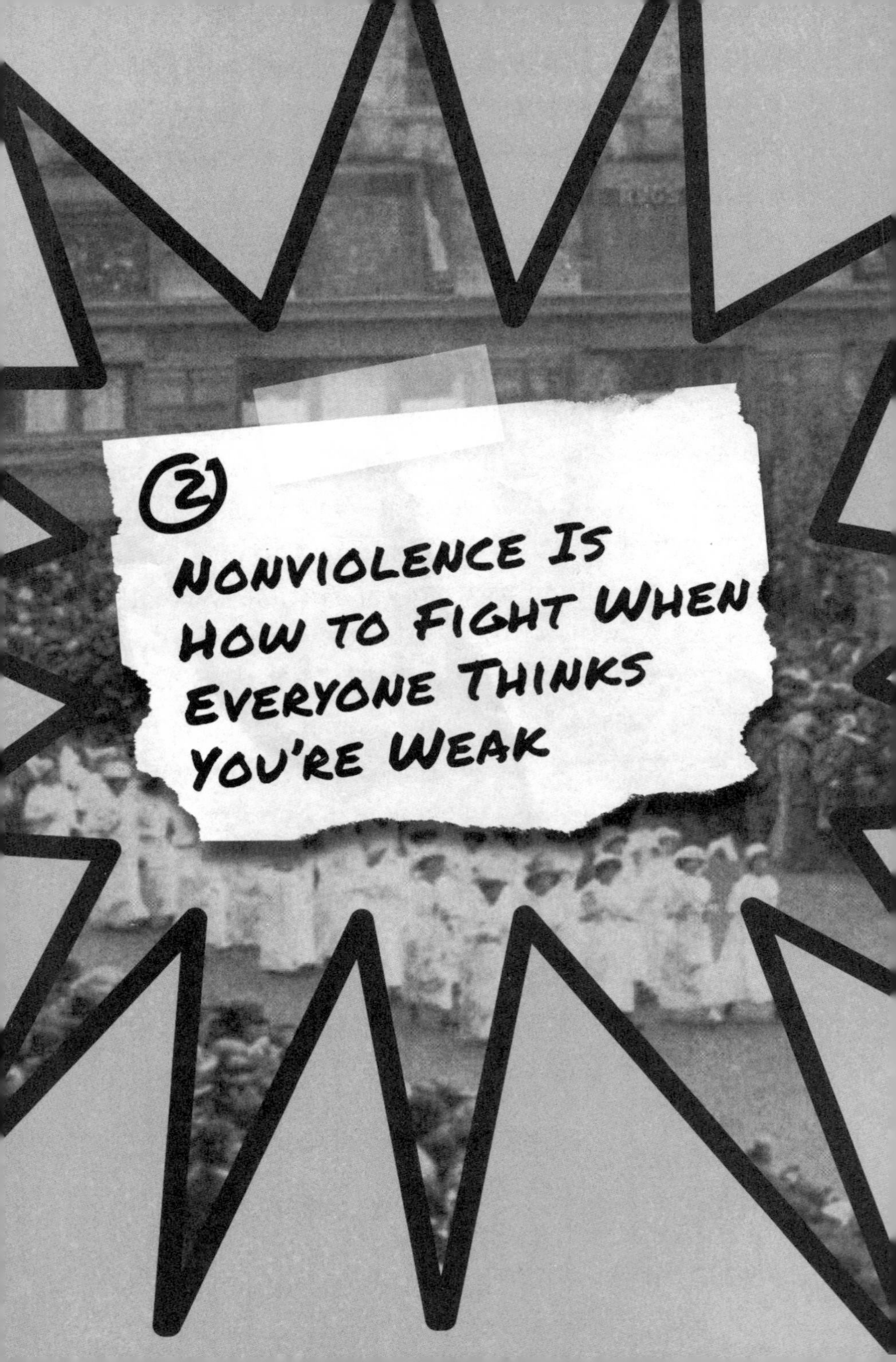
2
Nonviolence Is How to Fight When Everyone Thinks You're Weak

Alice Paul, who led the final charge for woman's suffrage, in 1915

ALICE PAUL and VOTES for WOMEN

> **"History had taught us that no great reform could hope to succeed without a downright fight . . . not necessarily a fight with arms; perhaps merely with brains, wits, and devoted sacrifice, but a real fight."**
>
> —Doris Stevens

THE WOMAN HOLDING THE BANNER IN THIS PICTURE IS Alice Paul, leader of the American suffrage movement. She appears gaunt and haggard. Her cheeks are sunken. Her dark eyes are half closed. Her face is nearly expressionless. There doesn't seem to be much of her under that hat and heavy jacket. She may, of course, be raising this banner, but it almost seems as if she can't lift its weight.

Three months before this picture was taken on October 20, 1917, Paul collapsed from exhaustion and spent a month, some of it in the hospital, recovering. She was so sickly that one doctor thought she might only have weeks to live. Paul was notorious for working too hard for too long. For neither eating nor resting enough.

There Is But One Choice. Alice Paul takes the fight to President Wilson in 1917.

This photograph shows that she still hadn't regained her full strength.

She looks weak.

A hundred years ago, many would look at this picture of what appears to be a weak woman and not be surprised. Back then it was commonly believed women were weak; just another way in which women were less than men.

Many used this belief to deny women the right to vote. Some argued that women were physically too weak to withstand politics' demands. One anti-suffrage pamphlet invoked "physiological facts" to support its claim that "women could not undertake the physical responsibilities of enforcing any law, which, by their votes, they might cause to be enacted."

Such people, some of whom were women, would see this picture of Alice Paul and say, "Of course she looks weak. She *is* weak."

But was she?

Paul's banner reads:

THE TIME
HAS COME TO
CONQUER OR SUBMIT.
FOR US
THERE IS BUT
ONE CHOICE.
WE HAVE MADE IT.
President Wilson

President Woodrow Wilson originally made this statement to justify the United States' decision to enter World War I in the spring of 1917. Three years after the war in Europe first began, Wilson concluded that our country could no longer remain on the sidelines. THE TIME HAS COME. America could fight the Germans, or yield to them. TO CONQUER OR SUBMIT. These were our options. But in actuality yielding could never be America's route; there weren't two choices after all. FOR US THERE IS BUT ONE CHOICE. The United States, by joining the war, announced its decision. WE HAVE MADE IT.

President Wilson's sentences are direct and powerful. They express determination in the face of a simple, but monumental, choice.

Alice Paul appropriates the president's words, boldly reapplying them to express something quite different. She isn't addressing the war. Instead, Paul is using Wilson's language to support a different cause: a woman's right to vote. This fight had been going on since the middle of the previous century, when a few hundred women in Seneca Falls in upstate New York first demanded this right. But recently this conflict has escalated. Women have been arrested and sent to jail. The price of the fight has steadily increased.

So Paul, like Wilson, has a decision to make on this October day. Fight on or give in. Conquer or submit. Back away from conflict or step further into the fray, knowing full well the cost of battling the most powerful man in the United States, along with the rest of the political establishment he represents.

Paul has made her choice.

On October 20, 1917, Alice Paul walks to the White House and raises this banner, with the intention of getting herself arrested. She will succeed and will be sentenced to seven months in prison.

Incredibly, a little over a month later, after sacrificing even more while behind bars, after enduring incredible suffering, it is Wilson who will submit to her.

A weak woman?

Hardly.

Alice Paul was not the first woman to carry a banner for suffrage.

Ten months earlier, on January 9, three hundred suffragists packed the East Room, the largest room in the White House, for a memorial. They were there to honor Inez Milholland, who had recently died at the age of thirty-one. Milholland, who suffered from an "erratic heart," had been sent out west to campaign for suffrage in the November elections. During her demanding travels—she was to appear in more than thirty cities in a single month—she came down with a bad infection, and never recovered. Her tragic death transformed her into a martyr for the cause, and the delegation hoped President Wilson, now preparing for his second term in office, would finally be moved by her sacrifice to support a national amendment granting women the right to vote.

Sara Bard Field, a suffragist from California, addressed the president: “How long, how long, must this struggle go on?”

But Wilson deflected their plea. Despite telling Field and the rest of the suffragists that he personally supported their cause, he offered an excuse. “As the leader of a Party, my commands come from that Party, and not from my private personal convictions.”

In other words, the president of the United States claimed he took his orders from the Democratic Party.

This was nonsense. At the very least, Wilson had the power to announce publicly that the time had come to support, and vote on, a national amendment.

Wilson turned and left the room.

The women—stunned, dejected, and angry—walked the short distance from 1600 Pennsylvania Avenue to Cameron House, the headquarters of the National Woman’s Party (NWP), to take stock of their situation.

By 1917, the fight for suffrage was almost seventy years old. What began as a small gathering in Seneca Falls in 1848 was now a massive national movement. Supporting suffrage had become a mainstream idea, and a number of states had even changed their laws to give women the vote in national elections. This progress was the result of steady, determined, institutional activism. Generations of women had given lectures, signed petitions, held conventions, raised funds, published editorials, lobbied government officials, organized local suffrage chapters, and educated any American, man or woman, willing to listen.

But the final goal, a national amendment to the U.S. Constitution granting all American women the vote, remained elusive. Over and over, women were told to wait. In addition, the president, senators, congressmen, and other powerful men assured them that their demands would be met in time, so long as suffragists continued employing their polite, ladylike tactics.

The women at Cameron House were done with all that.

Harriot Stanton Blatch—whose mother, Elizabeth Cady Stanton, first called for a woman's right to vote at Seneca Falls back in 1848—spoke up boldly: "We have got to take a new departure . . . We have got to bring to the President, individually, day by day, week in and week out, the idea that great numbers of women want to be free, will be free, and want to know what he is going to do about it. Won't you come and join us in standing day after day at the gates of the White House with banners asking, 'What will you do, Mr. President, for one-half the people of this nation?'"

At ten o'clock the next morning, twelve women stepped out of Cameron House. They wore sashes of purple, white, and gold, the colors of the suffrage movement. Each woman held a long pole, from the end of which hung a giant banner. Eight banners contained stripes of the suffrage colors, while the other four displayed a message. The women walked in single file across Lafayette Square and Pennsylvania Avenue before four colored banners and two lettered banners came to a stop at both the east and west gates of the White House.

They took their positions and raised their banners high. The messages read:

MR. PRESIDENT WHAT WILL YOU DO FOR WOMAN SUFFRAGE

MR. PRESIDENT HOW LONG MUST WOMEN WAIT FOR LIBERTY

The Silent Sentinels, as these and similar protesters came to be known, were the first Americans ever to picket the White House. They would stand before the president's home seven hours a day, six days a week, no matter the weather, for most of 1917 and into 1918.

Alice Paul, the leader of the Sentinels, organized the pickets using military language, because this peaceful act was designed to create conflict. She gave out "General Orders," and referred to herself as "Commandant," while various suffragists would act as "Officer of the Day." "Privates" had "Morning Detail," when only the "Sergeant of the Guard" was allowed to communicate with the press.

The Sentinels received elaborate instructions on how to respond to police interference. They were given

A Simple, Peaceful Weapon. The banners of the Silent Sentinels, who stood outside the White House day after day, month after month, spoke volumes.

a detailed list of alternate locations to occupy near the gates if forced to move. A last resort would be to march from gate to gate, but under no circumstances were they to fight back.

Over the course of a year, some two thousand women would take turns holding banners, whose messages changed constantly. These women hailed from virtually every state in the nation, though most lived along the East Coast. They tended to be educated and come from wealthy families, but there were working-class women and immigrants among them as well. Most were in their twenties or thirties, yet some were much, much older.

What they all had in common was not only the belief that President Wilson needed to be confronted, but also the willingness to challenge him publicly day in and day out, for long hours, whatever the weather. Their intense commitment to the cause of women's suffrage took them away from their homes, their families, and their careers. Challenging the president publicly opened them to ridicule and, in time, much worse.

The banner was the suffragists' answer to their apparent powerlessness. These women couldn't simply force those in power to give them what they wanted, at least not violently. In 1919, Doris Stevens, a leading suffragist of the time, listed "every known scientific device" used "to annihilate the enemy." She mentioned bayonets, poison gas, tanks, and much more.

"We could not and would not fight with such weapons," Stevens wrote. "How could we, with reasonable speed, rout the enemy without weapons, and we a class without power and recognition? Our simple, peaceful, almost quaint device was a BANNER!"

As these first Sentinels took their positions by White House gates, a new chapter in the fight for women's suffrage began. Over the next few years their banners took these and many other brave women from those gates to police stations, courtrooms, jails, and, finally, the voting booth.

•

The path leading to the Silent Sentinels began in the fall of 1907. In November of that year, Alice Paul attended a talk in Birmingham, England, given by Christabel Pankhurst on women's suffrage. Paul, just twenty-two years old and not yet an activist, had recently arrived in England, having come there to continue her studies and practice social work. She believed in a woman's right to vote, but this was not yet her cause.

Pankhurst's talk changed all that, though not because of anything she said. In fact, Paul barely heard her at all, as the men in attendance "sang, yelled, whistled, blew horns" and "played rattles etc from beginning to end." Sitting in this raucous hall, surrounded by men who thought ridicule was the proper response to a woman demanding her right to vote, Paul may well have realized, for the first time, the limits she would face in life. She had been raised in a tight-knit Quaker community in Morristown, New Jersey, where girls were educated just like boys and women were considered men's equals. Paul had graduated top of her class and went on to Swarthmore College, where she excelled again.

As such, Paul had largely been spared the reality of women's second-class status. But this painful truth was clear to her now. Only five years older than Paul, Pankhurst had trained as a lawyer but was not allowed to practice because of her gender. Paul entertained becoming a professor. How in the world would she find a respected place in that male-dominated world?

Her eyes suddenly opened, Paul soon joined the Women's Social and Political Union (WSPU), a radical organization headed by Pankhurst's mother, Emmeline. The WSPU was fed up with the slow progress made by other suffrage groups, a sentiment clearly expressed in their rallying cry: "Deeds, not Words." True to their slogan they employed confrontational, militant tactics, such as shouting down government officials and interrupting political meetings, acts that often led to their imprisonment. Over the next year, Paul gradually became a "heart and soul convert" to their cause.

On the evening of June 29, 1909, Paul joined one of sixteen groups of women—so-called deputations that contained around ten women each—carefully organized by the Pankhursts to demand a meeting with Prime Minister H. H. Asquith, an opponent of women's suffrage. Anticipating a violent encounter with police, the women wore "papier-mache armor" under their clothes for protection, or, in Paul's case, "black ropes of spinners' cotton wool." The first deputation of women marched on the Parliament building, itself surrounded by a clamorous crowd of fifty thousand onlookers who had come to watch the well-publicized showdown. As the women approached Parliament they were met by a massive police barricade. The police informed the women that Prime Minister Asquith refused to meet with them and ordered the activists to leave. But the women did no such thing. Instead, the other fifteen groups of women joined, one at a time.

Deputation by deputation the show down intensified.

Paul described the "awful scene," saying it was "a wonder that no one was killed" in this violent confrontation between the activists and the police:

> The suffragettes threw themselves against the lines of police & forced their way through once or twice only to be captured in a few minutes. Behind them was the crowd yelling & shouting & pushing them on but afraid to take any part for fear of being arrested. The police grabbed the suffragettes by the throats & threw them flat on their backs over & over again.

Paul herself was arrested for the first of many times in her life that evening. After the police took her and dozens of other women away, a separate group of

WSPU activists hurled stones through the windows of nearby government buildings.

In jail, Alice Paul struck up a conversation with an arrested woman wearing an American flag pin on her lapel. It belonged to Lucy Burns, another idealistic American swept up in the Pankhursts' movement, who would become Paul's right-hand woman in the years to come. Burns's warmth and charm perfectly complimented Paul's smoldering intensity. Together they would prove to be a potent team.

In the following months, Paul worked full-time for the WSPU. Her daring, her commitment, and her willingness to risk her well-being for the movement increased by the day. While in England, she would experience ten arrests and three stays in prison. Paul even joined other imprisoned suffragists in a hunger strike, so authorities brutally force-fed her fifty-five times. She described the hideous experience:

> One of the doctors stood behind & pulled my head back till it was parallel with the ground. He held it in this position by means of a towel drawn tightly around the throat & when I tried to move, he drew the towel so tight that it compressed the windpipe & made it almost impossible to breathe—

> with his other hand he held my chin in a rigid position. Then the other doctor put the tube down through the nostril. When they have finally secured you in this position you can scarcely budge.

A mixture of raw eggs and milk would then be poured down the tube. Often the tube would be bloody when removed.

The Pankhursts taught Alice Paul many lessons. They taught her how to organize, how to inspire others, and how to publicize a cause. But most of all they taught Paul to fight for what she believed in, even if it meant sacrifice and suffering.

In 1910 Alice Paul returned to the United States. Despite all she experienced in England, Paul was still considering an academic career and wouldn't return to full-time activism for another two years. Instead she completed her PhD at the University of Pennsylvania, writing on women's legal inequality. She officially joined the American movement near the end of 1912 and quickly emerged as a leader.

Finally committing once and for all to suffrage activism was a crucial decision. But as Paul became an influential figure within the movement, a second decision awaited her: What methods would she employ? Back in England she was, in her words, "just a little stone in a big mosaic." She apprenticed under the Pankhursts and did as they said; never questioning their tactics, no matter how extreme. But as a leader she would be more than a larger stone; she would be the craftswoman who designed the entire work.

The WSPU's confrontational tactics invigorated Paul, but she wouldn't merely copy their methods. Instead, in her second crucial decision, she chose to lead nonviolently. This choice was anything but arbitrary, as Paul drew from the nonviolent spiritual tradition of her childhood. She was a Quaker, a member of a small religious group that first broke off from the Church of England approximately 350 years ago. These early Quakers were pacifists and believed that violence could never be justified. The authorities persecuted them for their antiwar stance, and in response many Quakers immigrated to the new colonies across the ocean to find religious freedom.

Alice Paul was raised a pacifist and educated about Quakers who maintained the "peace witness" during early American wars by refusing to bear arms. Many Quakers were jailed for these beliefs.

Far from home in England and thrilled by the

Pankhursts' militancy, Paul clearly strayed from her Quaker upbringing.

But this would prove temporary.

From its beginnings, being a Quaker meant choosing a "testimony" or reform goal, one that would allow a person to work for social justice. In 1656, the founder of Quakerism, George Fox, described testimony as being "valiant for the Truth upon earth," a phrase that echoes the translation of Gandhi's satyagraha: holding firm to truth. Alice Paul would eventually choose for herself an ambitious testimony: creating lasting change in America by winning women political rights.

But just as important as the goal of Paul's testimony was its method.

According to Quaker beliefs, both goals and methods must be based on a clear moral vision. It was in part for this reason that Paul, once back in the United States, crafted a nonviolent campaign, one that steadily diverged from the increasingly violent WSPU struggle. As she wrote in 1913, her movement was to be part of a "process of Moral evolution."

Despite the differences between the American movement and the Pankhursts, critics of both often use the term "militant" to describe those tactics they considered inappropriate for women. Paul did not reject this label, but redefined it instead: "It is not militant in the sense that it means physical violence. It is militant only in the sense that it is strong, positive, and energetic."

Paul also had practical reasons for rejecting the Pankhursts' violence: their destructive acts made it easy for their opponents to vilify them and their followers. More than this, she sensed that using exclusively nonviolent tactics might just give the weak access to incredible strength.

Overall, Paul combined elements of Quaker pacifism and Pankhurst militancy in such a way as to *avoid violence but welcome conflict*, a distinction that perfectly explains the philosophy of nonviolent struggle in general. Two scholars, referring to a dozen nonviolent movements spread across the twentieth century, perfectly describe activists like Paul: They "did not come to make peace. They came to fight."

In 1912 Alice Paul became head of the Congressional Committee (CC), a small arm of the leading suffrage organization in the United States, the National American Woman Suffrage Association (NAWSA). The CC's mission was to advocate for a national amendment to the U.S. Constitution that would give women the vote. But the CC was little more than an afterthought in 1912, because NAWSA's main focus was on their so-called "state by state" strategy. Instead of aiming to amend the country's constitution, NAWSA worked to get individual states to alter their own laws. Unfortunately, not one of the twenty most populous states had yet enfranchised its women. Meanwhile, the CC had a tiny annual budget, some of which had been returned, unused, the previous year.

Nevertheless, Paul—young, determined, and a bit naive—believed that a national amendment to the U.S. Constitution could be won within a year. After consulting with Lucy Burns, the two decided on their first big event: a suffrage parade in Washington, D.C. They chose March 2, 1913, as the date, because the following day Woodrow Wilson would be inaugurated as the twenty-eighth president of the United States. Wilson was a native of nearby Virginia, and Paul hoped to take advantage of the huge crowds in town for the occasion.

But why a parade?

A little over a hundred years ago, a procession, especially a large one, was a proven method for getting exposure. And as Paul learned from her time in England, women marching in public was still a radical act. Marching was the stuff of armies, and armies were male. When women took to the street they questioned what it meant to be ladylike and challenged the literal place of women in public. A large, orderly procession of women marching through the nation's capital would force people to reconsider the very relationship between women and power.

But there were a few problems with this plan. The inauguration was barely three months away, they had no budget to speak of, and next to no one committed to march.

Nevertheless, they got to work, as Paul began demonstrating the single-minded devotion to suffrage and women's rights that would characterize the rest of her life. During her years as a leader of the suffrage movement, Paul had no personal life whatsoever. As a journalist wrote about her in 1919, "There is no Alice Paul. There is suffrage. She leads by being . . . her cause."

Paul worked day and night to make this procession a reality. She raised funds, recruited participants from around the country, and organized volunteers to put in long hours with her at the new Washington, D.C., office. Other suffragists were inspired by her example, but none could match it. As one exasperated activist would write: "Miss Paul neither eats and many times

I do not believe she sleeps, but if she does she dreams about the Federal Amendment."

On March 2, Woodrow Wilson traveled by train from Princeton, New Jersey, to Washington, D.C. He expected to be greeted by a large crowd of supporters, but instead he looked around confused at the mostly deserted Union Station and asked, "Where are the people?"

"Oh, they are out watching the suffrage parade," he was told.

At two thirty sharp, eight thousand women—led by the striking Inez Milholland, who wore a cape and crown and rode atop a white horse—would pass before a quarter of a million onlookers.

What motivated thousands of women to travel to the nation's capital in order to march? Without a doubt, the situation for American women in 1913 was much better than in 1848, when the movement first began. To take just one example, more and more women were now working outside the home, which would seem to give them greater economic independence. However, this independence was often hard to achieve due to discriminatory laws. For instance, a 1908 Supreme Court decision ruled that states could restrict the number of hours a woman could work per week, so that women would still have enough energy to perform their "maternal functions." Such laws limited a woman's effort to control her own life. Women encountered similarly incomplete progress everywhere, from marriage laws to college admissions practices.

Overall, these marchers—factory seamstresses from New York, schoolteachers from Kansas, college students from California—understood that conditions for women had improved, but needed to improve much more. And there was one tool they could all use to challenge the injustice and discrimination all women faced: the vote.

With the sounds of musicians rehearsing, early motorcars rumbling loudly, and horses clacking down the avenue, the CC leadership divided the marchers into state delegations, college groups, and professional organizations. They all lined up behind a massive yellow banner that read:

WE DEMAND AN AMENDMENT TO THE CONSTITUTION OF THIS UNITED STATES ENFRANCHISING THE WOMEN OF THIS COUNTRY

The scene was awash in colors. Floats, chariots, costumes, marching bands, sashes, capes, and, of course, American flags turned the nation's capital into a veritable rainbow. These women believed that beauty and power can and should coexist.

Two hundred marshals instructed the women "to march steadily in a dignified manner." They were not to talk or wave to the crowd, because this procession was designed to challenge the assumption that women lacked discipline. The suffragists prepared to march along the same street that Wilson, in his own parade from which women were barred, would travel down the next day.

Or so they planned.

As it turned out, many of the men lining the streets were not supporters. Just the opposite. They came to the parade to mock and taunt the marchers. Nellie Mark, a physician from Baltimore who came to march, said that she "never heard such vulgar, obscene, scurrilous, abusive language." Soon after the procession was finally set in motion down Pennsylvania Avenue, the border between parade and crowd dissolved. The women were pressed so tightly together that they couldn't march at all.

Then things got worse.

The men, many of them drunk, grabbed banners, threw lit cigarettes, pushed, pinched, and even slapped the women. And just as the police had allowed these men to cross the cables lining the streets meant to separate the crowd from the marchers, most of those in uniform did nothing to stop these attacks. In fact, numerous police were smiling and making lewd comments themselves.

Eventually the chief of police was forced to call in federal cavalry troops from Fort Myer in Maryland. They took over an hour to reach the chaotic scene. In the meantime, ambulances carried the injured women away. Approximately a hundred of them would require emergency room treatment.

Alice Paul had no illusions about why the event spun out of control. "It was meant to happen," she told a reporter the following day. "That was all there was to it. The police could have stopped the disorder instantly. They had only to be determined about it."

Paul might have sounded angry or disappointed, but in fact she was thrilled. She understood a central truth of nonviolent activism: an event violently interrupted by the opposition is many times more useful than one allowed to proceed peacefully. The parade was not a "catastrophe, but an unlooked-for blessing." As Paul explained a week later, "This mistreatment by the police was probably the best thing that could have happened to us, as it aroused a great deal of public indignation and sympathy."

The women had been attacked on the streets of the nation's capital for doing nothing more than marching peacefully.

Their readiness to suffer—more important, their refusal to fight back—did not go unnoticed by a potential ally with an even bigger voice: the press.

"Police Must Face Charges," the *Fort Wayne Sentinel* wrote, while the *Washington Post* characterized the confrontations as "little less than riots."

Public opinion quickly turned, and the Senate, on the very day of Wilson's inauguration, voted to investigate police action during the march.

Paul's original hope for the parade was a large turnout and newspaper coverage the next day. Instead the movement benefited from two weeks of congressional hearings, as no less than one hundred and fifty people testified about what they had endured. In the end, the Washington, D.C., chief of police lost his job, while the demand for the so-called Anthony Amendment, which would give women the right to vote, was back on the front pages of the nation's newspapers.

Where Paul intended to keep it.

•

Alice Paul and four well-connected suffragists next managed to arrange a meeting with President Wilson. The president, thirty years older than Paul and a one-time college professor, arranged five seats in a semicircle facing his chair in the Oval Office, as if he intended to hold class. But it was Paul who would soon teach him a lesson.

Suffrage is "the paramount issue of the day," Paul told the president.

Wilson claimed he had no opinion on the matter.

He then changed the subject to various issues he was eager to work on with Congress: currency revision and tariff reform. The president likely expected the meeting to soon end, the bothersome suffragists grateful he had agreed to meet with them at all.

Rather than leave, Paul said, "But Mr. President, do you not understand that the Administration has no right to legislate for currency, tariff, and any other reform without first getting the consent of women?"

Paul's words bluntly explained to the president why she described her cause as "paramount" to begin with. In her eyes, the American government was illegitimate as long as half its adult population was barred from elections. Paul's readiness for confrontation, during her very first meeting with the president, shows how this young suffragist was anything but meek.

Paul believed that winning President Wilson's support for a constitutional amendment was the key to its success, and she and her followers would employ a variety of methods in the coming years to persuade him. They held more parades and sent group after group to lobby Wilson and his Democratic counterparts, who were a majority in Congress. When this didn't work, these women formed their own political party. The National Woman's Party (NWP) campaigned *against* Democrats in those states where women could already vote, in order to punish them for failing to support a national amendment.

And when all these tactics failed to bring results, the Silent Sentinels were born.

For the first few months of 1917, the Sentinels picketed the White House without incident. The tactic won them steady publicity, and they soon became a tourist attraction for those visiting the nation's capital. The president took to nodding, smiling, waving, or tipping his hat when passing them each day.

Otherwise, he ignored them.

To be fair, there was something even bigger stubbornly demanding Wilson's attention at this time: World War I.

•

The United States entered the war on April 6, 1917. As is almost always the case during wartime, the public and press called for everyone, suffragists included, to support the war effort and put everything else on hold. And the more compliant NAWSA did just that, with their leader, Carrie Chapman Catt, writing to Wilson that "it seemed to us only fair to you to wait yet a while longer and not press for suffrage during this extraordinary session."

But those aligned with Alice Paul refused such obedience, because they viewed the president's rationale for joining the war as hypocritical. President Wilson promised the United States would make the world "safe for democracy." But how could the United States champion democracy abroad if back home its own democracy excluded every other person of voting age?

Not only did the Sentinels remain by the White House gates, the language of their banners now directly challenged the president's reasoning for war. DEMOCRACY MUST BEGIN AT HOME, one read.

From the beginning of the pickets, Paul and the Sentinels regularly changed the banners' messages in order to guarantee steady publicity. Just changing the words was good, but employing bolder and bolder language in order to escalate the confrontation was even better.

On June 20, the day a group of Russian allies visited the White House, the Sentinels took the showdown between themselves and the president to a new level. As the Russians drove through the gates, Lucy Burns and Dora Lewis held aloft a banner addressed to the diplomats:

PRESIDENT WILSON AND ENVOY ROOT ARE DECEIVING RUSSIA. WE WOMEN OF AMERICA TELL YOU THAT AMERICA IS NOT A DEMOCRACY. TWENTY MILLION AMERICAN WOMEN ARE DENIED THE RIGHT TO VOTE. PRESIDENT WILSON IS THE CHIEF OPPONENT OF THEIR NATIONAL ENFRANCHISEMENT. HELP US MAKE OUR GOVERNMENT REALLY FREE. TELL OUR GOVERNMENT THAT IT MUST LIBERATE ITS PEOPLE BEFORE IT CAN CLAIM FREE RUSSIA AS AN ALLY.

The assembled crowd reacted angrily to what they viewed as a deeply unpatriotic act. One man tore part of the banner from its frame, and then others leapt forward to finish the job, ripping what was left to shreds.

Burns and Lewis continued standing with nothing but wooden poles in their hands.

As planned, the incident got more attention in the press than the actual visit of the Russians to the White House.

The next morning the picketers returned with a duplicate version of the Russian banner and were greeted by a much larger, even angrier crowd. Some boys destroyed the banner before the eyes of passive policemen.

More Sentinels followed with other banners, including Hazel Hunkins, bearing a message that read WE DEMAND DEMOCRACY AND SELF GOVERNMENT IN OUR OWN LAND.

Hunkins was spat at.

Her banner grabbed and trampled on.

Hunkins was wrestled to the sidewalk. But, as one historian puts it, she "countered her instincts to fight back." Hunkins herself wrote to her mother that she responded as Alice Paul had instructed her to: like "a non-resistant pacifist and not an offender in any way."

After over a half year of the Sentinels picketing undisturbed, Major Raymond Pullman, Washington, D.C.'s chief of police, suddenly informed them that they would be arrested if they continued.

"Why has picketing suddenly become illegal?" Paul asked. "Our lawyers have assured us all along that picketing was legal. Certainly it is as legal in June as in January."

Pullman repeated his warning.

"The picketing will go on as usual," Paul replied.

Paul knew that technically the law was on their side, but she understood that in practice, picketing would now be treated as civil disobedience, as a deliberate violation of police orders.

Not a single suffragist had been arrested since Paul's return to the United States. Would she ask her fellow activists to sacrifice their personal freedom for an even greater one?

On June 22, Mabel Vernon, Lucy Burns, and Katharine Morey all walked separately to the White House. None of them had exited Cameron House with a banner, though Vernon had carried out a box with her. When the three of them eventually met up at the east gate, Vernon opened the box and handed the other two its contents: a banner, this one containing Wilson's own words:

WE SHALL FIGHT FOR THE THINGS WE HAVE ALWAYS HELD NEAREST TO OUR HEARTS,

A Silent Escalation. The Sentinels showed their devotion to the cause by continuing to picket even after it was deemed illegal.

FOR DEMOCRACY, FOR THE RIGHT OF THOSE WHO SUBMIT TO AUTHORITY TO HAVE A VOICE IN THEIR OWN GOVERNMENT

After insulting him and essentially calling him a liar the day before, they now turned the president's language against him.

The three police present were dumbfounded. "Them's the President's own words," one said.

The police had clear orders to arrest any picketers, but how could quoting Wilson himself possibly be unlawful? The confused trio eventually concluded that they had no choice but to act on the commands they were given. Burns and Morey refused to surrender their banner and were arrested.

The charge?

Obstructing traffic.

Those first charges against Burns and Morey were dropped, but almost a week later six suffragists were brought to court under the same bogus charges. They each were fined $25.

But the women refused to pay and publicly rejected the court's unjust verdict. "Not a dollar of your fine shall we pay," the six said. "To pay a fine would be an admission of guilt. We are innocent."

The judge sent them off to serve three days in the district jail, making them the first American women to go to prison for demanding the right to vote.

And so the summer of 1917 ushered in a new routine: pickets, arrests, trials, and jail sentences. The NWP, relying on the power of its numbers, showed it had no shortage of banners to display or women to send to prison. Again and again the convicted suffragists used the courtroom as an opportunity to call out the true reason for their arrests: "We know full well," said Mrs. John Rodgers Jr., a direct descendent of Roger Sherman, one of the signers of the Declaration of Independence, "that we stand here because the President of the United States refuses to give liberty to American women." In mid-July, sixteen suffragists were sentenced to sixty days in the Occoquan Workhouse, where the women found rat-infested cells and a menu of inedible foods: stale bread, sour soup, and rotten meat. Worms riddled every dish.

Word leaked out about the terrible conditions under which the jailed Sentinels were kept, and after only three days Wilson himself pardoned the new inmates. It appeared that future picketers might not be arrested at all. But the newly freed suffragists received this good news around the same time they got an ominous warning from the highly feared superintendent of Occoquan, Raymond Whittaker: "The next lot of women who come here won't be treated with the same consideration that these women were."

The first imprisonments in Occoquan gave the suffragists another wave of sympathetic publicity and brought about positive action in Congress. The Senate woman suffrage committee, whose task it was to consider and possibly vote on the Anthony Amendment, issued its first favorable report not long after some of its members visited the prisoners there. The House of

Representatives finally set up a similar committee of its own.

The NWP's strategy seemed to be getting results, and so on Friday, August 10, the Sentinels chose to escalate the confrontation between themselves and the president yet again. Lucy Burns brought a new banner to the White House:

KAISER WILSON HAVE YOU FORGOTTEN HOW YOU SYMPATHIZED WITH THE POOR GERMANS BECAUSE THEY WERE NOT SELF-GOVERNED? 20,000,000 AMERICAN WOMEN ARE NOT SELF-GOVERNED.

Kaiser was the title of the enemy German leader, making this banner the most scandalous yet and showing that these activists, however nonviolent, weren't about to pull any punches. A man grabbed Burns's banner and ran off, but otherwise police kept order at the scene.

On Monday, three more "Kaiser" banners were taken to the White House gates. All were torn down. The following day, August 14, the picketers couldn't even reach 1600 Pennsylvania Avenue. The furious crowd, heavily populated with servicemen and numbering at least a thousand, attacked NWP headquarters, where they destroyed every banner they could get their hands on.

After locking the doors to Cameron House, Lucy Burns, Virginia Arnold, and Elizabeth Stuyvesant grabbed some remaining banners, ran up to the second and third floors, and hung them from the balconies. In response, three sailors found a ladder in an adjacent theater, climbed to the second-floor balcony, and tore them down. When Burns went onto the balcony, she was nearly pulled over the railing, struggling for her life against the sailors as the transfixed crowd watched from below. A sailor punched one young suffragist right in the face. The violent mob pelted the headquarters with eggs, tomatoes, and stones. A bullet even shot through the building. As afternoon turned to evening, the police, who had looked on idly for hours, finally stepped in and regained order.

The following day Paul joined the pickets, which once more turned violent. She was knocked down three times and dragged thirty feet along the pavement by a sailor. Other Sentinels were attacked as well. The police went back and forth between keeping order and joining the attackers. By midweek approximately 150 banners had been seized or destroyed. Worse yet, the women were informed that if they continued picketing the arrests would begin again.

Alice Paul faced a difficult decision. On the one hand, she believed that it was necessary to keep pressure on President Wilson. On the other, it was impossible to ignore the fact that this recent escalation had cost them some goodwill. The Sentinels' "treasonous" acts were now turning public opinion against them.

Despite this the confrontational pickets continued. As did the arrests and trips to jail.

As summer turned to fall in 1917, Paul understood that only the women's ongoing suffering could garner sympathy and advance the cause. But not just anyone's sacrifice would be enough at this stage; it was time for another escalation. In regular wars, generals remain safe while foot soldiers trade shots and risk their lives on the front lines miles away. But in a nonviolent struggle, things work differently. Here the leader herself would have to face danger directly if she were to challenge power.

The head of the NWP decided that it was time for her to go to prison.

On October 20, Paul carried a banner bearing the words of the president once again: THE TIME HAS COME

TO CONQUER OR SUBMIT. FOR US THERE CAN BE BUT ONE CHOICE. WE HAVE MADE IT. She was arrested and given a seven-month sentence. Before this no suffragist had been sentenced to more than sixty days.

In prison Paul began a hunger strike. If each and every nonviolent tactic exists somewhere along a spectrum—from easy and safe on one side, to difficult and dangerous on the other—then hunger striking lies at the far edge of the difficult, dangerous end. This most extreme tactic demands of the activist a willingness to suffer immensely and even risk her life.

Paul had gone on a hunger strike back in England, so she knew full well the torment for which she was volunteering. In 1909, after first using the tactic, she had written in a letter to her mother, "I shall *never* go on a hunger strike again."

As had been the case in England, it was likely the American authorities would respond by force-feeding her, since they could not afford to have a prisoner die of starvation while in their custody. And the American force-feedings would turn out to be even worse than those of the British, since here it was performed three times a day. Back in England they only did it twice.

Paul responded by demanding political prisoner status, claiming that she was unfairly arrested because of her political protest against an unfair government, and not because she broke any laws.

Not content with force-feeding her, Paul's jailers soon placed her on a stretcher and carried her to the psychiatric ward, where no one, not even her lawyer, could visit her. There Paul was checked regularly by a Doctor J. A. Gannon in order to determine if she was in fact mentally ill. If Gannon settled on a diagnosis of insanity, he could transfer her to St. Elizabeth's, a government-run insane asylum, where she might be held indefinitely, well beyond the duration of her sentence. A hundred years ago "difficult," but otherwise sane, women were often sent to asylums to be isolated and thus silenced. In such a place Paul would be removed from the legal system altogether and rendered utterly powerless.

Any optimism Paul had that Gannon was a regular doctor concerned only with his patient's well-being was dashed when he told her, "I will show you who rules this place."

In order to weaken her further, boards were nailed over the windows. Throughout the night, a nurse woke her each hour by shining a bright light in her face, leading to sleep deprivation, a classic torture technique.

"I believe I have never in my life before feared

anything or any human being," Paul said later. "But I confess I was afraid of Dr. Gannon."

Despite all this, Paul never broke.

Meanwhile the Sentinels continued their protests. Before her arrest, Paul had planned to increase the picketing in order to send women to prison in "such numbers that the government cannot handle the situation."

Instead of a handful of women, dozens of suffragists—intentionally recruited from all across the country so that news of their treatment would reach far and wide—stood at the White House gates and were soon arrested. Just as in a traditional war, in which the side with more soldiers often prevails, the suffragists were now employing their abundant numbers with an eye on exhausting their opponent. Only, this time around the battlefields were the gates of the White House, the courts of Washington, D.C., and the jail and prisons surrounding it. The government had plenty of experience commanding a regular army, but the NWP showed that it had the organization, the resources, and, above all, the committed soldiers to successfully wage this unconventional war on its own terms.

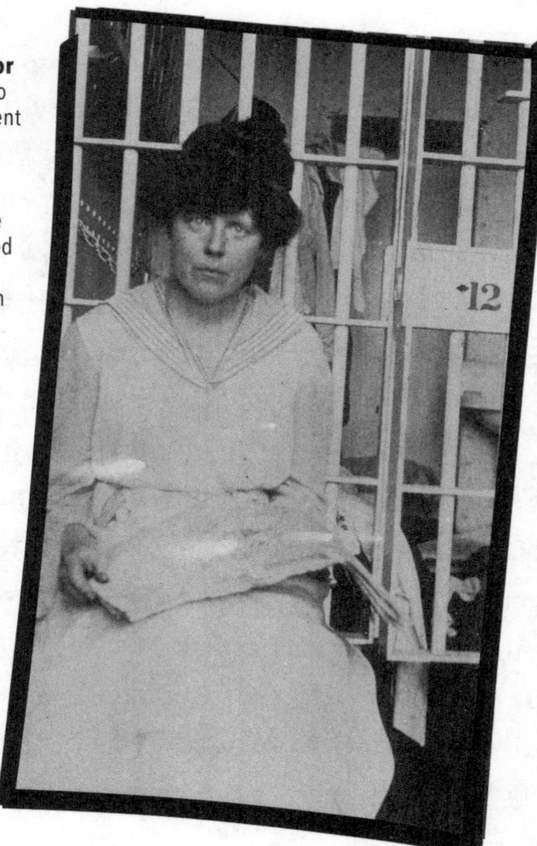

Suffering for Suffrage. No suffragist spent more time in prison than Lucy Burns, pictured here in the dreaded Occoquan Workhouse in 1917.

A perplexed judge freed the first wave of women brought to his court, but when most of them returned after being arrested again just a few days later, he began handing out sentences. The thirty-one convicted women were supposed to be sent to district jail, but their final destination turned out to be Occoquan instead.

The women arrived there late in the evening on November 17. A couple hours after their arrival, while the new inmates were waiting in a holding room, a furious Superintendent Whittaker, with his "blazing little eyes," burst in. When Dora Lewis, acting as spokeswoman for the group, informed Whittaker that they wanted political prisoner status, he told her, "Shut up. Sit down." When she did not, he ordered two guards to take her away.

Whittaker was about to act on the threat he had made to the women months earlier. Moments later the room filled with men, some not even in uniform, wielding clubs.

Women were dragged and tossed into small, dark, dank cells. Dorothy Day was thrown down twice over an iron bench. Dora Lewis was knocked unconscious. Alice Cosu suffered a heart attack but wasn't attended to for hours. The women were threatened with straight-jackets and gags; others were beaten and choked. When Lucy Burns began calling out the names of each woman to make sure they were okay, she was handcuffed to the bars of the cell, her arms held well above her head for hours. Whittaker was overheard saying that Lewis and Burns should be sent to solitary for life, if not killed.

The women began a hunger strike of their own the next day. In response, the superintendent moved the inmates from room to room in apparent random order so that they might succumb to disorientation. Force-feedings followed.

Soon news of the women's treatment began leaking out. On November 23, at a hearing about the legality of sending the suffragists to Occoquan in the first place, the weakened prisoners, some of whom hadn't eaten for days, were presented to a concerned judge and observed by alarmed members of the press. The judge had them transferred to the district jail, where Paul remained on hunger strike. Thanks to the hard work of her lawyer, she had recently been released from the psychiatric ward and placed in the prison hospital.

Within days of the women's transfer to the district jail, an unexpected visitor came to see Alice Paul. He was let into her room at 9:00 p.m., even though official visiting hours were long since over. The visitor was the journalist David Lawrence, a close friend of Woodrow Wilson, whom Lawrence first got to know as a student back at Princeton. Lawrence claimed to have come on his own and not at the request of the administration, but it appears he was in fact there to negotiate with Paul on behalf of the president himself. They spoke for two hours in her room.

Lawrence asked if the suffragists intended to resume their picketing.

Paul responded that this would "depend upon the

attitude the Administration and Congress seemed to be taking toward the Federal Amendment."

Lawrence next addressed the matter of the thirty or so hunger strikers, who were still demanding political prisoner status. Lawrence told her that it would be "the easiest thing in the world" for the administration to grant them such status. They could be moved to a "fine house in Washington" and be given "the best of food." The only problem with this idea was that it might encourage other Americans who opposed America's entrance into the war to demand the same. This could not be permitted, and therefore "it would be easier to give you the Suffrage Amendment than to treat you as political prisoners." As such, Lawrence informed Paul that the president would "make it known to the leaders of Congress that he wanted it passed and would see that it passed."

Instead of claiming he took orders from the party, as he had done earlier, President Wilson was now ready to act on his authority as the most powerful man in the American government.

Lawrence said that the suffrage bill would be taken up soon, but it might take two sessions of Congress before it went through both houses.

Negotiating forcefully, despite almost certainly being bedridden as well, Paul told Lawrence that the NWP would not be satisfied with that timetable.

The visitor left.

On November 27 and 28, all the suffragists, including Paul herself, were suddenly released with no explanation.

The recently freed Paul, who hadn't eaten voluntarily for three weeks, said: "We are put out of jail as we were put into jail, at the whim of the Government. They tried to terrorize and suppress us. They could not, so they freed us."

This conversation, the freeing of the jailed Sentinels, and, most of all, Wilson's decision to publicly support the Anthony Amendment, demonstrated the power the "weak" actually possess. These suffragists were able to perform what scholars of nonviolence call "political jiujitsu." Jiujitsu is a form of martial arts designed around the idea that a smaller, weaker opponent, with the proper technique, can in fact defeat a bigger, stronger opponent by using their opponent's great, unruly force against them to throw them off balance.

The government had the authority to arrest and jail these women. It even had the power to restrain them physically and force-feed them.

But the suffragists turned the government's tactics against them.

With each application of their power, the police, the judges, the politicians, and the president himself unwittingly escalated an ongoing conflict in which they looked worse and worse at every step. The suffragists' willingness to suffer again and again made the president look less like a champion of democracy abroad and more like a despot at home. Paul clearly understood this back-and-forth jiujitsu dynamic quite well when she spoke to reporters after being freed: "We hope that no more demonstrations will be necessary. But what we do depends entirely upon what the Administration does."

Wilson seemed to have all the control, but ultimately it was the suffragists who forced the president of the United States down to the ground, until he had no choice but to agree to their demands.

The weak had transformed into the mighty.

The suffragists didn't get their amendment right away. Though Wilson had finally agreed to endorse their cause, it would take some time before all of Congress fell in line behind him. The House of Representatives acted quickly, approving the Nineteenth Amendment on January 10, 1918, but the Senate would take much longer. The women lobbied senators and kept the pressure on Wilson, who remained reluctant to become a consistent advocate for this change to the Constitution.

The suffragists created new tactics to force the president's ongoing support, like lighting a fire in a Grecian

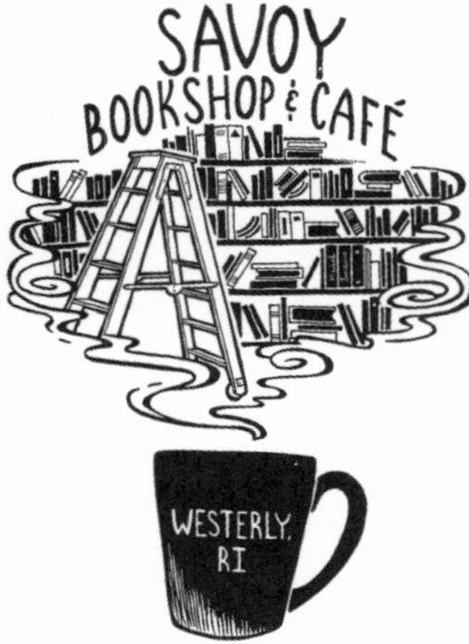
SAVOY
BOOKSHOP & CAFÉ
WESTERLY, RI

LOCALLY OWNED

FIERCELY INDEPENDENT

BANK SQUARE BOOKS
MYSTIC, CT

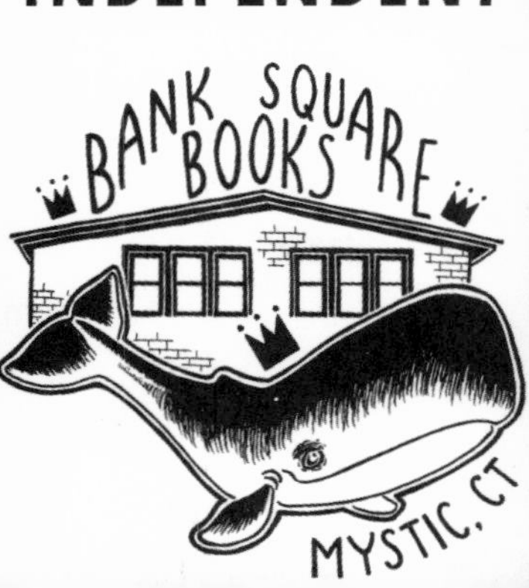

SAVOY BOOKSHOP & CAFÉ

10 CANAL STREET
WESTERLY, RI 02891
401-213-3901

savoy@mysticbooksinc.com

savoybookshopcafe

savoybookshopcafe

BANK SQUARE BOOKS

53 WEST MAIN STREET
MYSTIC, CT
860-536-3795

bsb@mysticbooksinc.com

banksquarebooks

banksquarebooks

urn in front of the White House and burning his words in it. There were additional arrests and trips to jail. By the end of their last protest, 500 women had been arrested and 186 sent to jail. On June 4, 1919, the Senate finally followed the House's lead. The amendment then went to the state level for ratification. By the narrowest of margins, the Tennessee House of Representatives ratified the amendment on August 18, 1920, making it the thirty-sixth state to do so, the number necessary at that time to finally alter the U.S. Constitution.

That November, with the Nineteenth Amendment now in place, millions upon millions of women, including Alice Paul, voted for the very first time.

To be sure, Paul and the NWP cannot be given all the credit for this achievement. From 1913 to 1920, Carrie Chapman Catt and NAWSA also worked tirelessly to advocate for women's suffrage. Thanks to their efforts, more than a dozen states amended their own laws to enfranchise women before 1920. Both organizations continued the long, slow process, started seventy-two years earlier, of convincing Americans that women deserve the right to vote, and this gradual change among the average citizen influenced the elected officials who represented them.

Even though they were often at odds with one

another, when it came to strategy—NAWSA rejected all confrontational tactics, sticking instead to institutional methods like petitions and lobbying—the NWP needed NAWSA and vice versa. Nevertheless, what seems undeniable is that the nonviolent struggle led by Alice Paul jump-started a stalled movement and accelerated the passage of a national amendment by many years.

More than this, Paul's bold and courageous methods helped women not merely gain the vote, but reinvent the way they saw themselves as well. Just as Gandhi led his people toward a new and better view of Indian identity—independent and no longer submissive—so Paul propelled women to reconsider what it meant to be a woman in the first place. As two scholars put it:

> Paul was trying to alter the prevailing view of women: as weak, insufficiently educated, hysterical or temperamental, dependent on men, and not worthy of the vote. Instead of being hampered by actual limitations, Paul believed, women were hampered by inaccurate views of their own capabilities. With a new sense of self-respect, they could achieve all: they could become American heroes.

Paul showed that women could forge this new identity through nonviolent resistance.

Winning the vote certainly mattered to her, but in truth Paul's ambition extended to include something much greater: a reworking of femininity itself.

Though sexism still remains a stubborn problem in today's America, women in this country can marry who they want when they want, choose their own career path, live independently, and, in a million ways big and small, be precisely the kind of woman they want to be. Alice Paul and the suffragists hardly started this ongoing process, but it's undeniable they gave it a great and lasting push forward.

By practicing nonviolent resistance, the Silent Sentinels demonstrated to a nation that quality these women had in themselves all along: boundless, steadfast strength.

But would these same strategies work for those who weren't just dismissed as worthless, but were in fact virulently hated for the color of their skin? Could nonviolent activism prove that love really is stronger than hate?

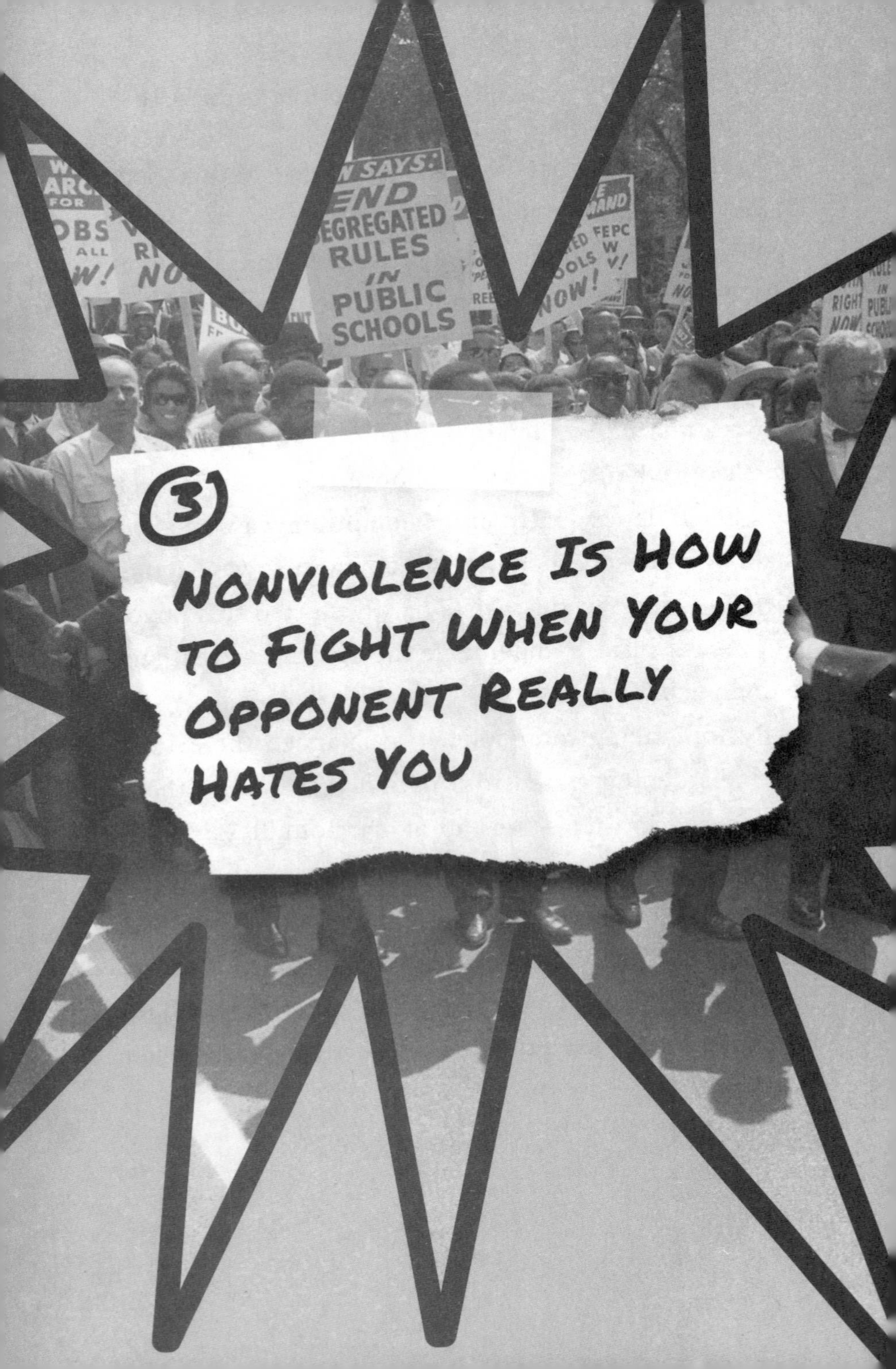

③ Nonviolence Is How to Fight When Your Opponent Really Hates You

MARTIN LUTHER KING JR. and PROJECT C

Martin Luther King Jr., who changed a nation with his words and actions, speaking in 1965

"The only weapon we have in our hands . . . is the weapon of protest. That's all."

—MARTIN LUTHER KING JR.

THE PHONE RANG IN THE MONTGOMERY, ALABAMA, HOME of Martin Luther King Jr. late one night near the end of January 1956. King had moved there a little more than a year before to become pastor of the Dexter Avenue Baptist Church, but now he was the leader of the Montgomery Bus Boycott as well. This mass action started in early December, sparked by Rosa Parks's refusal to stand up for a white passenger and move to the back of the bus. Since then the entire black population of the city had been boycotting the bus system in order to pressure the white authorities to rescind segregation for all riders.

"Listen, nigger," an unknown voice said on the other end of the line, "we've taken all we want from you. Before next week you'll be sorry you ever came to Montgomery."

His wife, Coretta, and their first child, born in November, were sleeping not far away.

King was barely twenty-seven years old. The inexperienced pastor had been selected to lead the boycott in large part because he was so new to town he hadn't yet gotten mixed up in any of the infighting so common within Montgomery's African American community.

This threat was hardly an isolated incident. Since the start of the boycott, the phone rang constantly at King's home, anonymous racists calling to insult him and his family. Dozens of nasty letters arrived each day containing similar sentiments. Worse yet, a white contact had informed King that reliable sources believed plans were afoot to kill him.

Only the day before, King had been arrested for driving thirty in a twenty-five-miles-per-hour zone. On his way to jail, uncertain that this was in fact his destination and overcome by the hatred directed at him day after day after day, King feared he was about to be lynched.

Tonight's call was finally more than he could handle. After hanging up on the menacing voice and sitting with a cup of coffee, King became paralyzed by an overwhelming, boundless fear. All alone he prayed at the kitchen table. "I am afraid . . . I am at the end of my powers. I have nothing left. I've come to the point where I can't face it alone."

King then heard a divine inner voice, one telling him: "Stand up for righteousness, stand up for truth; and God will be at your side forever."

Hearing those words and no longer feeling alone, King was able to overcome his fears and continue leading the boycott.

Through his faith, Martin Luther King Jr. summoned the strength to endure the hatred directed at him day in and day out. Yet he wanted to do more than just tolerate this vitriol, he wanted to combat it, he wanted ultimately to transform this society built on it.

But how?

Through nonviolent resistance.

Martin Luther King Jr. embraced nonviolence for many of the same reasons Gandhi had before him. King saw nonviolent resistance as a strategy of the courageous, not the cowardly, of the active, not the passive. For King, nonviolence was the way for an oppressed people to challenge their oppression without contributing more violence themselves.

Living in the American South—where blacks weren't

just oppressed, but often openly and viciously hated as well—the philosophy of nonviolence resonated powerfully for King. To King, nonviolence meant battling hate with love, meant believing that love was ultimately stronger than hate, and meant hoping that through nonviolent activism a community deformed by hate could be repaired. King believed, like Gandhi before him, that nonviolence could lead to justice and not just the defeat of one's opponent.

King's belief in the power of love, and of loving one's enemies especially, stemmed from his Christian faith. In the New Testament, Jesus said, "Love your enemies, do good to those who hate you."

But for King this religious tradition didn't mean suffering for suffering's sake. He liked to quote some lesser-known words of Jesus, who also said, "I have not come to bring peace, but a sword." Of course, Jesus did not mean a literal sword, but rather a belief in the necessity of conflict when faced with injustice.

For Jesus and Gandhi, and now King, too, nonviolent action was the right way to fight a battle one cannot and should not walk away from.

King was not the first African American leader to adopt Gandhi as a teacher and a guide. Benjamin Mays and

Mordecai Johnson, two pastors a generation older than King, each visited India separately and were inspired by Gandhi's message. They both played a role in introducing the younger King to Gandhi's work years before he reached Alabama.

By the start of the Montgomery Bus Boycott, King was already a proponent of nonviolent resistance, but his commitment to its philosophy was still incomplete, his understanding of its strategies and tactics uneven. King's training continued under the guidance of Bayard Rustin, who had been practicing nonviolent activism since the early 1940s.

Rustin—who, like Alice Paul, based some of his beliefs in nonviolence on his Quaker upbringing—believed in nonviolence so deeply that once, at a protest against the Korean War in the 1950s, an outraged passerby grabbed Rustin's picket sign in order to beat him with its stick. Rustin's response? He handed the man a second stick to use on him, too.

In February 1956, Rustin drove alone from New York to Montgomery to witness the bus boycott for himself. He was immediately impressed by the community's enthusiasm and dedication. The boycott, which many had expected to quickly collapse, was still going strong. Rustin saw in King a leader of unusual promise, but the movement itself was still too intimate with the practice of violence. Armed guards stood watch outside King's home, and guns were everywhere in his house. During Rustin's first visit to the residence, he overheard the minister shouting to a guest not to sit down on a particular couch, as there was a loaded weapon resting on it.

Rustin reached out to his contacts in New York, in particular the Fellowship of Reconciliation, a pacifist organization whose members included some of the first Americans to embrace Gandhi's teachings, and implored them to send experts in nonviolence to Montgomery. Glenn Smiley, a white civil rights leader and Gandhi follower, was sent to Montgomery to further King's training.

With their thorough understanding of Gandhi's methods, Rustin and Smiley didn't believe that nonviolent action would spare blacks from white violence. But they sensed that only an unwavering commitment to nonviolent methods could prevent the outbreak and escalation of widespread violence on all sides once blacks started resisting segregation on a mass scale. They convinced King that he must do everything in his power to make the movement he led purely nonviolent.

After all, large parts of the American South at this time weren't just deeply racist, they were violently racist. Whites had lynched more than four thousand blacks since the end of the Civil War, and the slightest offense was more than enough to trigger horrific, lethal acts. Just half a year earlier, Emmett Till, a fourteen-year-old African American from Chicago visiting his family in Mississippi, was brutally murdered for supposedly flirting with a white woman. None of the killers went to jail for this crime, despite a trial that included eye witnesses for the prosecution.

King's teachers and soon King himself came to believe that a truly nonviolent movement—well-organized and highly disciplined—could end segregation.

But how?

Nonviolent resistance would be met by violent racist suppression. The inevitable suffering of civil rights activists would thus expose the true brutality and vicious cruelty at the heart of segregation for all the nation and world to see.

Three days after the late-night phone call, King's house was bombed. Even then, with irate and armed supporters ready to charge the police barricade nearby, King was able to calm his flock. Standing on the porch of his home with arms raised, King told the outraged crowd, a few hundred in number, "If you have weapons, take them home . . . We are not advocating violence. We want to love our enemies . . . We must meet hate with love."

In the face of a potentially lethal attack on not just him but his family as well, King stood firm in his belief that nonviolence was the only answer.

But could African Americans use nonviolent resistance to defeat segregation?

Could love truly overcome hate?

In the Jim Crow South, a black person—from the separate hospital in which he was born to the separate cemetery in which he was buried—could live his entire life experiencing scant contact with whites. Schools, parks, theaters, restaurants, drinking fountains, stores, pools, and bus stations, they were all "separate but equal."

But of course, this equality was a lie. African Americans got less of everything, and what they got was almost always worse, too. The city of Birmingham, Alabama, for instance, spent twice as much per white student than it did for each black student.

A 1954 Supreme Court decision, *Brown v. Board of Education*, finally ruled that separate but equal was unconstitutional. The opponents of segregation had won a major legal victory, but this didn't mean that segregation would suddenly disappear. No, communities would have to be forced to integrate.

The yearlong Montgomery Bus Boycott was a key early effort in making the white community accept integration. It ended on December 20, 1956, when a federal court, following the 1954 decision in *Brown*, ruled that bus segregation was unconstitutional. This ruling, combined with the power of the boycott itself, made bus desegregation a reality. The following day Rosa Parks rode up front, legally.

The success of the boycott brought Martin Luther King Jr. fame, energized opponents of segregation throughout the South, and demonstrated the power of nonviolent activism. But the coming years didn't quite deliver on the great promise of Montgomery. After all, there were dozens of cities like Montgomery across the South, and in every one segregation expressed itself in a variety of ways. Where to focus? What to target? And how best to organize the thousands upon thousands of people willing to fight this deep-rooted discrimination?

Numerous organizations sprouted up, activists were trained, and the African American leadership, including King, pressured the federal government to act.

But progress was slow.

Again and again, King was called upon to join a campaign that had already begun, one started by other activists. In late 1961, he found himself in Albany, Georgia, where efforts to challenge segregation and register black voters were met by a sly sheriff, Laurie Pritchett, who over and over found ways to neutralize nonviolent tactics. Pritchett ordered his police to avoid violence themselves, at least when journalists were present, and had many of those arrested sent to jail in other communities, in order to prevent prison overcrowding. By summer 1962, the city's authorities had simply outlasted the activists and King left town, where, as the *New York Times* put it, "not a single racial barrier fell."

King was frustrated, but not about to give up. In fact, he was determined to apply the hard lessons he learned in Albany.

But others weren't so sure.

Maybe Montgomery was a fluke.

Maybe King was in over his head.

Maybe nonviolent action had no real chance of defeating segregation nationwide.

The movement, along with King himself, needed a victory, and soon.

•

"Birmingham is where it's at, gentlemen. I assure you, if you come to Birmingham, we will not only gain prestige but really shake the country. If you win in Birmingham, as Birmingham goes, so goes the nation."

These were the words of Fred Shuttlesworth, a prominent minister and dedicated activist who knew the ugliness of Birmingham, Alabama, as well as anyone. Shuttlesworth had been bravely fighting segregation in the city for seven years, and had paid a stiff price for doing so. His home had been bombed twice, while his and his wife's effort to enroll their children in a white elementary school led to him being beaten with bats and chains just outside the building, a ruthless attack in which his wife was stabbed.

Birmingham was the largest city in the state of Alabama, and may well have been the nation's capital of segregation and violent racism. The Ku Klux Klan, with its eleven thousand members in the Birmingham area, had deep ties to the police and the city government. The city commission was so racist that in 1961 it voted to close more than one hundred city parks and playgrounds rather than integrate them.

Even worse, more than fifty black homes in Birmingham had been bombed since the late 1940s, with no one ever prosecuted. One neighborhood had been targeted so regularly the locals referred to it as Dynamite Hill, while they called the city itself Bombingham. As King put it, Birmingham was "by far the worst big city in the US as far as race relations go."

Though Birmingham was hardly the easiest target in their effort to desegregate the South, King and his team nevertheless chose the city for a new campaign, knowing how great the reward would be if they could somehow succeed.

On January 10, 1963, King and ten others gathered in secrecy at a retreat in Dorchester, Georgia. They were there to fine tune their plans for Project C.

"C" stood for "confrontation."

The first lesson these activists took from Albany was the need to be in charge from the very beginning. They would no longer join a campaign already underway. The Dorchester group—which included King; his right-hand man, Ralph Abernathy; James Lawson, an expert in training nonviolent activists; and Wyatt Walker, who drafted the blueprint for the coming campaign—would choose not just the place, Birmingham, but the exact timing and the specific tactics as well.

Nonviolent resistance had a reputation as a spontaneous phenomenon, something as unpredictable as the weather. A bunch of people would grow outraged and suddenly take to the streets. The aim of Project C was not merely to overturn segregation in Birmingham, but also to demonstrate that different methods of nonviolent direct action could be coordinated in advance to achieve maximum effect.

Much like generals gathered in their headquarters and huddled over the map of a future battlefield, these leaders considered every tactic at their disposal and every obstacle they might face. Walker's planning was so meticulous he knew precisely how long it would take activists of different ages and physical abilities to walk from the Sixteenth Street Baptist Church, Project C's staging area, to various segregated lunch counters in downtown Birmingham.

Project C was to have four phases: sit-ins, boycotts, mass marches, and, finally, an influx of outsiders who would reinforce the local activists. The ultimate aim was to "cripple the city under the combined pressure of publicity, economic boycott, and the burden of overflowing jails." The stages were to be timed in such a way as to steadily increase the force of the campaign, to create, in King's words, "a situation so crisis-packed" that the "pus-flowing ugliness" of segregation would burst open for all to see.

Project C wasn't merely ambitious, it would be dangerous as well. The notorious Bull Connor had headed the Birmingham police force for most of the previous quarter century. Connor was a die-hard segregationist, determined to combat the civil rights movement no matter what it took. Two years earlier, in spring 1961, a group of white and black activists, known as the Freedom Riders, rode throughout the South to challenge the illegal segregation of interstate bus lines. As they reached the Birmingham bus terminal on May 14, Connor allowed local KKK members—who brought baseball bats, iron pipes, and chains with them—to have fifteen minutes alone with the riders before sending in the police. The violence spun out of control so quickly that seven innocent bystanders wound up in the hospital.

When asked why the police were slow to arrive, Connor responded that they were honoring Mother's Day with their mothers.

King ended the Dorchester meeting by sharing a sober observation: "There are eleven people here assessing the type of enemy we're going to face. I have to tell you that in my judgment, some of the people sitting here today will not come back alive from this campaign. And I want you to think about it."

Project C was launched on April 3, 1963, also known as B-Day. Sixty-five activists, prepped by Walker on logistics and by King and Lawson on nonviolence, split off into five groups and made their way to some of Birmingham's segregated lunch counters. The organizers were hoping for closer to three hundred volunteers, but sixty-five would have to do.

Unfortunately, most of the lunch counters, rather than deal directly with the activists, simply shut off their lights and closed down for the day. Only one location, Britt's, called in the police. Twenty-one activists were arrested.

The remainder of the first week didn't go much better, with less than a hundred volunteers going to jail. Meanwhile, not only was virtually all of white Birmingham opposed to the campaign, many blacks were, too. A recent city election promised to bring a new mayor into office, a supposed moderate who would improve race relations and the place of blacks in the city. The Project C leadership was pressured to call the whole thing off. But the campaign stubbornly kept on. As Shuttlesworth put it, "We're tired of waiting. We've been waiting 340 years."

In the short term, however, their determination didn't pay off, and by April 10 the campaign was in deep trouble. Fewer than 150 activists were in jail. Fewer and fewer people were attending nightly mass meetings at the church, where fewer and fewer people were volunteering to risk arrest the following day. The national press, whose coverage was desperately needed, seemed to be losing interest entirely.

Hoping to finish off the stalled campaign altogether, Connor served King with an injunction, prohibiting him from engaging in any acts of protest. Even marching would now be illegal for him and the other 132 individuals named in the court order. Things were looking so bleak that King would later reflect that "our most dedicated and devoted leaders were overwhelmed by a feeling of hopelessness."

Nevertheless, King decided he'd march anyway. Only fifty volunteers agreed to join their leaders. King had no idea how his arrest might help, but he went anyway, calling his decision a "faith act." Connor's men arrested him and the others, placing King in solitary confinement, where he had to sleep on metal slats.

In the dim silence of "the hole," King was left with nothing to do and no way to do it. After months of intense planning and recruiting, all with the aim of mobilizing an entire community to challenge segregation, the leader of the campaign now found himself utterly alone. He could do little but read the newspapers smuggled in to him. The news, obviously, wasn't good, but an article in the *Birmingham News* about white clergymen condemning the demonstrations as "unwise and untimely" upset him the most. A man of words as well as action, King picked up a pen and wrote a response in and around the margins of this and other papers, using arrows to clarify the movement of his snaking prose.

Once he started writing, King could not stop. In a "universal voice, beyond time, beyond race," King detailed the insult, the poverty, the hatred, the cruelty, the pain, the brutality, and the murderous violence out of which black life in America had been built generation after generation. King's "Letter from a Birmingham Jail" stands today as a document of incredible force, as a profound, eloquent justification for what was then a largely unpopular struggle. Many of its words still ring true: "Injustice anywhere is a threat to justice everywhere." "The time is always ripe to do right." "Oppressed people cannot remain oppressed forever."

All the same, this letter did not save Project C. In fact, throughout the rest of April, Wyatt Walker couldn't find a single major newspaper or magazine willing to print it. Only in mid-May, once the campaign was essentially over, did mainstream publications like the

New York Post and the *Atlantic Monthly* begin to show interest and help the letter find the mass audience it would eventually reach.

Project C would save King's letter, transforming "King's letter from a silent cry of desperate hope to a famous pronouncement of moral triumph."

But what saved Project C? With its leadership in jail, commitment flagging, and interest nonexistent, who would create the crisis the movement needed?

Children.

Jim Bevel motored into Birmingham in his 1959 Rambler from Greenwood, Mississippi, on April 12, the day of King's arrest. King had summoned the younger preacher, who had attended the January meeting in Dorchester, where he had said little.

Which isn't to say that Bevel was timid. Anything but. Bevel was a fiery veteran of the Nashville sit-in campaign of 1960 that successfully integrated the city's lunch counters, and something of a maverick as well. He had come to nonviolence slowly and reluctantly, resisting the pleas of his seminary hall mate, the great nonviolent activist and future congressman John Lewis, for the better part of a year. Before choosing the seminary, Bevel had a rock 'n' roll recording contract,

Radical Leadership. James Bevel, pictured here with Martin Luther King Jr., gave Project C a much-needed shot in the arm.

and even after he found religion he remained bold and brazen, eccentric and unpredictable. When he reached Birmingham his head was shaven, upon which sat a yarmulke, a head covering worn by observant Jews. Bevel was not actually Jewish, but he had great respect for the religion and said, "I consider myself a rabbi." Of course, this might not have been the only reason he covered his head in such a manner. Bevel may also have been wearing a yarmulke because the site of a black man with one so confused southern police that they tended to leave him alone.

Bevel spoke at the mass meeting that evening. The campaign was in desperate need of encouragement, of some morale boosting. But the twenty-six-year-old preacher in denim overalls laid into his audience instead. After announcing that the crowd of three hundred was pitifully small, the "spiritual kamikaze" declared "Birmingham is sick." "Some Negroes don't want to get well," Bevel sneered at the locals. "If they do, they would have to compete with the white man. There are some negroes who want segregation as much as Bull Connor."

Bevel verbally attacked the white police detectives in the church, too, calling them "white trash" and challenging them directly: "You can put me in jail but you can't stop us." Turning back to the blacks he had just insulted, he now sought to energize them. "The police can come to our meeting, bring their guns and their badges and little microphones to church," he continued, "but if you want to be free, there is nothing they can do about it . . . The negro has been sitting here dead for three hundred years. It is time he got up and walked."

Wyatt Walker followed Bevel at the podium, where he floated a radical tactic by asking the youth to volunteer to march. "Some of these students say they have to got to go to school," Walker said, "but they will get more education in five days in the City Jail than they will get in five months in a segregated school."

While Project C continued to falter (there were fewer than forty-five arrests in the last ten days of April), Bevel, along with other leaders like Andrew Young and Dorothy Cotton, held afternoon workshops for students. In the basement of the Sixteenth Street Baptist Church, the young activists underwent nonviolence's version of basic training.

Their education began by learning a fundamental tenet of nonviolence, something the Indian independence movement illustrated in the aftermath of the Salt March: the oppressor's power requires the consent of the oppressed. Bevel told them:

> You are responsible for segregation, you and your parents, because you have not stood up . . . No one has the power to oppress you if you don't cooperate. So if you say you are oppressed, then you are acknowledging that you are in league with the oppressor; now, it's your responsibility to break the league with him.

Once students understood why they had to take action, they were trained in how exactly to challenge the authorities. These young people learned everything from what to say if police demanded that they identify their parents ("No comment," in order to spare the adults from retaliation) to how to protect themselves if fire hoses were used to disperse them (curl up like a ball and cover your head with your hands).

To toughen them up in preparation for the abusive treatment they'd encounter beyond the walls of the church, they role-played. Bevel and the other teachers shouted racist insults, including "nigger," at the students over and over again. The verbal assaults were matched by physical attacks, as the students were spat on and even hit. The teens trained themselves not to respond, summoning the strength to endure these humiliating, painful experiences and the discipline not to retaliate.

Finally, the students had to take an oath of nonviolence. If they couldn't make this vow, they would not be allowed to participate in protests. These trainees even had to sign a pledge form that listed the Ten Commandments of Nonviolence, which included rules like "REFRAIN from the violence of fist, tongue, or heart" and "REMEMBER that the nonviolent movement in Birmingham seeks justice and reconciliation—not victory."

As Bernard Lafayette, another teacher, put it, "This was a nonviolent academy, equivalent to West Point. We were warriors." And the ranks of this academy grew by the day, because when it came to attracting the young, Bevel was a Pied Piper. He understood that the best way to get young folks on board was to start with the most popular among them. He first recruited the top high school athletes, the prom queens, the students everyone else looked up to. They were enlisted in a whisper campaign, told to secretly spread the word about future workshops, as if openly joining might get a kid in trouble. The appeal of participating without the full knowledge of one's parents only made taking part that much more enticing.

More important, Bevel knew how to relate to teens, how to get them excited about joining something historic. Bevel would take his students to a graveyard and ask them to ponder the following: "In forty years you are going to be here. Now, what are you going to do while you're alive?" He understood that young people were relatively fearless compared to their parents. With jobs, home payments, and car loans, adults couldn't afford the risk of prison.

But kids could, and many of them eagerly would, if only given the chance.

Bevel was anxious to unleash his young foot soldiers onto the streets of Birmingham, but the rest of the campaign's leadership—including King, who was released from prison on April 20—wasn't so sure. In fact, many were vehemently opposed. Some argued that these kids, who ranged from about-to-graduate high school seniors to tiny third graders, couldn't possibly understand what they were volunteering for. Others worried that if children got hurt—let alone hurt badly—the adults who dispatched them would appear negligent, further undermining an already precarious campaign.

To make matters even more delicate, on April 30, Shuttlesworth's request for a parade permit was denied, meaning that simply marching would lead to arrest. Bevel finally convinced King to let the children protest by reminding him that personal salvation required only "conscious acceptance" of Christian faith. If a young child could make a choice about her eternal destiny, Bevel argued, how could she be refused the right to march?

King finally relented, perhaps because of Bevel's reasoning, but perhaps because he had simply run out of options. As Shuttlesworth put it, backing Bevel, "We got to use what we got."

At long last Bevel had approval to send his young soldiers into battle, though it seemed like he may have been planning to do so all along. Leaflets had already been circulating widely throughout Birmingham's black high schools. They instructed students, whether or not they received permission from their parents and teachers, to skip school and report to the Sixteenth Street Baptist Church by noon on Thursday, May 2. On May 1, Bevel and a local lieutenant who went by the nickname Meatball visited elementary schools to spread the word.

At that evening's mass meeting, Bevel declared, "We are going to break Birmingham wide open" and "give the employees of the Negro school a holiday tomorrow because the students are going to march."

The desperate strategy of the following day would make or break the Birmingham campaign, as well as King's reputation and perhaps even the civil rights movement as a whole. Knowing what lay in the balance, Bevel found a name suiting the moment, one borrowed from the riskiest and most decisive operation of World War II.

May 2 would be D-Day.

•

Thursday began with charismatic DJ Shelley the Playboy from black radio station WENN announcing to his listeners, "Kids, there's gonna be a party at the park." The park in question was Kelly Ingram Park, which lay kitty-corner from the church. Occupying a single city block, the normally quiet park was dotted with trees and crisscrossed by two diagonal sidewalks. Shelley continued: "Bring your toothbrushes because lunch will be served." With full knowledge of the coming action, Shelley reminded everyone to bring a toothbrush not because lunch would be served, but because having a toothbrush in jail is always a good idea.

Almost eight hundred students missed roll call that morning. And many of those who bothered to show up didn't stay for long. Student leaders took to the halls, passing by classrooms and calling out code words ("hayride," "sock hop," etc.) that signaled it was time to ditch class. At some schools the principals locked doors and gates, but the determined students slipped out windows and hopped over fences. By midmorning, Sixteenth Street Baptist Church was packed with children and teens shouting out the names of their schools, as if the whole thing were a giant pep rally.

At one o'clock the church doors swung open and

fifty youths, marching in two single-file lines, stepped out into the eighty-degree day. Many were clapping and singing an upbeat version of "We Shall Overcome." Others held signs with messages such as I'LL DIE TO

Power in (Young) Numbers. Thousands of African American youth went to prison as part of the "Children's Crusade," which transformed the conflict in Birmingham.

MAKE THIS LAND MY HOME and CAN A MAN LOVE GOD AND HATE HIS BROTHER.

The police, having gotten wind of a planned march, were already on the scene, and soon the first group of

marchers was loaded up into the nearest paddy wagon. They crammed in orderly, trained as they were not to resist arrest. Right around then, however, the church doors opened again, and another batch of fifty marchers headed out toward the park. They, too, were quickly taken into custody.

After a month of undersized protests, the police assumed that was it for the day.

They couldn't have been more wrong.

As soon as one group headed off to jail, another group emerged from the church. Actually, Bevel would wait just long enough to fool the police into thinking there were no more protesters left before opening the doors to set free another batch of young people. Soon the police were scrambling. Outnumbered, they lost track of some groups. More paddy wagons had to be called in. The county sheriff was contacted to send in his deputies.

A police officer spotted Shuttlesworth near the action. "Hey, Fred," he called out, "how many more have you got?"

"At least a thousand more," Shuttlesworth answered. He was exaggerating, but not by much.

"God Almighty," the policeman said.

With all the paddy wagons in use, school buses

arrived to transport the hundreds more who continued pouring steadily from the church.

The police, used to doling out cruelty to grown-up blacks, were thrown by the task of arresting mere children. One officer asked a girl her age as she climbed into a paddy wagon.

"Six," she answered.

By four o'clock that afternoon, six hundred young people were in jail, more than double the number of adults arrested throughout all of April.

Two thousand people attended a packed mass meeting a couple hours later. "The whole world is watching Birmingham tonight," Shuttlesworth announced proudly.

The "C" in Project C—Confrontation—was finally a reality.

But as successful as D-Day had been, King encouraged everyone not to rest on that day's success. Now was precisely the time to double their efforts. King inspired the crowd as he indirectly challenged the white authorities. "If they think today is the end of this, they will be badly mistaken."

When Bevel called for more volunteers, the atmosphere was so electric that three hundred people began marching up and down the aisles, impatient for tomorrow's arrival.

Meanwhile, hundreds of young activists sat in jail, where they were fed greasy, watery, unseasoned grits. Where they tried to sleep on mattresses without covers. Where they passed the first night of their incarceration crammed into cells designed for only eight prisoners with seventy-five other kids.

They would have no choice but to get used to the crowding. Many of their peers would soon join them.

Friday, May 3, Double D-Day as Bevel called it, started much like the day before. Fifteen hundred students skipped school, most of whom descended on the Sixteenth Street Baptist Church with an eye on joining their jailed classmates.

Before the day's marchers were sent on their way, a basket was passed around to collect anything that might be considered a weapon. The container was eventually filled halfway with knives, as some of the less disciplined young activists clearly needed an additional reminder that this campaign was and would remain nonviolent.

At one o'clock the first protesters emerged through the church doors. Their marching orders were a bit more complicated this time. Some smaller groups were sent in a new, different direction as a decoy, so that another larger group might have a chance of crossing the park and reaching Seventeenth Street, the border of white Birmingham, undisturbed.

But none of this planning mattered much. The jails were nearing capacity. Bull Connor's plan was to prevent today's marches while making minimal arrests.

The tool he would use to do this: the fire hose.

And not just a regular fire hose. The firemen assembled water cannons by joining together two hoses through a single nozzle, the entire apparatus mounted on a tripod. With the water pressure doubled, the new "monitor guns" could rip the bark off a tree from a hundred feet away.

After a quick warning to the young marchers to disperse "or you're going to get wet"—a call the singing activists ignored—the hoses were turned on. Protesters were soon tumbling down the sidewalk. Faces were bloodied, clothes were torn from people's bodies, which were slammed into the nearest immoveable object: a car, a tree, a brick wall. Fifteen-year-old Gwendolyn Sanders feared for her life as the water struck her. "The pressure from that hose was so great that it would knock your breath away."

At this moment, from his window office looking down on the park, A. G. Gaston, an African American millionaire businessman, was on the phone with David

Water as a Weapon. Hoping to end the marching altogether, Bull Connor had his men use "monitor guns" to disperse protesters.

Vann, a white lawyer. The two were among the many Birmingham moderates who opposed the protests, wishing King and the rest of those "outside agitators" would simply leave town and let the architects of slow reform do their work. But Gaston's stance was about to change.

"Lawyer Vann," Gaston exclaimed, "they've turned

the fire hoses on a little black girl. And they're rolling that girl right down the middle of the street. I can't talk to you now or ever. My people are out there fighting for their lives and my freedom. I have to go help them."

Charles Moore, a white photographer, was in Birmingham to cover the protests. Driving through the city that afternoon, Moore saw the fire hoses battering the protesters and told the driver: "Stop the car now." He hopped out and took a picture of twenty-one-year-old Mamie Chalmers—a chunk of whose hair would be shorn off her head by the water—and two others pinned up against a wall.

The scene was terrifying, but many protesters didn't back down. Some ignored their training and actually taunted the police instead. So Bull Connor called for another weapon in his arsenal. "Bring the dogs," he ordered.

Eight K-9 units, made up of German shepherds and their handlers, descended on the crowd, which was now a chaotic mix of young waterlogged protesters and other African Americans of all ages, including many worried parents, who had come to the park to witness the showdown.

Three teens were bitten badly enough that they wound up in the hospital.

Walter Gadsden, a high school sophomore with no interest in protesting, had come to the park as a spectator. But a policeman suddenly grabbed Gadsden's cardigan sweater while his dog, Leo, lunged, ripping Gadsden's clothes near his abdomen. Associated Press photographer Bill Hudson caught the moment on film.

In response to the white authorities' brutal methods, some of Birmingham's blacks, mostly older bystanders not trained by Bevel or Lawson, were turning to violence themselves. They threw bricks, rocks, and Coke bottles at the policemen and firemen. Bevel and other leaders directed their marchers away from this confrontation with the hopes of keeping their protest nonviolent.

At three o'clock Bevel met police in the church, where a thousand more protesters, locked inside by the authorities, were still waiting to march. A truce was agreed upon and Double D-Day came to a close.

The hoses were shut off.

The dogs were returned to their cages.

But the damage had been done. Birmingham, along with the rest of the South, was now firmly on the road toward integration.

Despite his intentions not to fill the jails any further, Connor and his men arrested another 250 young activists on May 3. The local prison system was buckling under a pressure that wasn't about to let up. Birmingham's black community, once divided over King's leadership and the wisdom of nonviolent direct action, was now firmly on his side after the day's dramatic events.

At that evening's mass meeting, he reassured the many, many concerned parents in attendance: "Your daughters and sons are in jail . . . Don't worry about them. They are suffering for what they believe, and they are suffering to make this nation a better nation."

Other speakers emphasized the need for the next day's marches—the announcement of which was met by raucous applause—to remain completely nonviolent. "We have a nonviolent movement," Andrew Young said, "but it's not nonviolent enough."

Young's call for exclusively nonviolent resistance wasn't based merely on some moral or spiritual ideal. This was a practical matter. The peaceful demonstrators—brilliant practitioners of the nonviolent jiujitsu, of turning the oppressor's force against him—had set a trap. Connor and his men—armed with hoses and dogs—had walked right into it.

But the white authorities, blinded by their racist hatred, still couldn't see the foolishness of their actions.

Unforgettable Images. Shocking photographs, like this one of a police dog lunging at Walter Gadsden, powerfully conveyed the violent essence of racial segregation in the South for all the world to see.

Indeed, they didn't think anything all that bad had happened on Friday. True, more kids went to jail and a handful of people wound up in the hospital. But no one was seriously hurt, and, as a matter of fact, two firemen, pelted by bricks, wound up in the hospital themselves. Whether they approved of it or not, the white residents of Birmingham knew that blacks had seen much, much worse when it came to racial terror.

But the rest of the nation had not.

The May 3 confrontation was nonviolent theater at its very finest. Photojournalists captured the conflict on film, TV producers sent the unforgettable images into living rooms across the country that evening, and editors printed them on the front pages of the leading newspapers, both national and international, the next morning. Many Americans knew that the system of segregation was the product of a racist society. But seeing these images of young, unarmed blacks slammed against walls by fire hoses and attacked by vicious German shepherds finally made clear to anyone willing to look that racism was more than just an abstract idea or a strongly held belief about the supposedly fundamental differences between whites and blacks.

In practice, racism was brutal violence.

The pus King had mentioned back in January during the Project C planning meeting had burst forth. And nonviolent direct action had pierced the thin layer of "law and order" keeping it out of view.

Bayard Rustin, who had completed King's training in nonviolence seven years earlier back in Montgomery, watched the news that evening in New York. He called it "television's greatest hour." With the help of the media, the protesters had exposed the justice of their cause by revealing the wickedness of their opponents. Or, as David Vann said, "It was a masterpiece of the use of media to explain a cause to the general public of the nation."

After all, it wasn't that Bull Connor and his men unrolled the fire hoses and uncaged the dogs to oppress Birmingham's blacks every day.

The system of segregation, typically unopposed, didn't require that. A little ruthless violence from time to time was enough to maintain the system, was enough to make segregation a southern tradition for many.

What these protesters did was expose the hatred behind segregation, and the brutality behind both. What must a person think about black children, doing nothing more than marching peacefully, to turn hoses on them and attack them with snarling dogs, all to maintain what he calls order?

President John F. Kennedy—a steady, but cautious, supporter of the civil rights movement—got right to the point when he said the picture of Walter Gadsden made him "sick."

May 3 was not the daily routine in Birmingham, but it was an expression of the city's essence.

An essence the entire world could now see.

•

Segregation in Birmingham had suffered a serious blow, but the movement wasn't about to let up. The marches continued on May 4, while President Kennedy sent Burke Marshall, assistant attorney general for civil rights, to the city in order to coordinate talks between the two sides. This was a tricky task, since there were currently no whites in Birmingham willing to speak directly to King.

A truce was called for Sunday, May 5, but Bevel and others chose to break it after Guy and Candie Carawan, white folk singers who had introduced the song "We Shall Overcome" to the movement, were arrested on the steps of New Pilgrim Baptist Church, where a mass meeting was to be held. Furious, Bevel took to the pulpit. "We're tired of this mess! Let's all get up!"

Soon some two thousand marchers were on their way to the nearby city jail, led not by Bevel but instead Charles Billups, a Birmingham pastor and longtime colleague of Shuttlesworth. Two blocks from the jail they encountered at least six water cannons arranged in a line against them. When Billups reached the hoses he neither turned around nor continued walking. Instead, he knelt, as a wave of kneeling spread steadily behind him.

After a prayer, Billups stood up and declared, "We're not turning back. We haven't done anything wrong. All we want is our freedom. How do you feel doing these things?" Tears now running down his face, Billups began a chant the others would soon join: "Turn on your water! Turn your dogs loose! We will stand here 'til we die!"

Bull Connor ordered his men to turn on the water. They did not. "Dammit! Turn on the hoses!" he ordered again.

Again they refused to obey.

Some firemen were now crying themselves. One responded to Connor, "You turn it on yourself. I am not going to do that."

Another said, "We're here to put out fires, not people."

"Let us proceed," Billups said.

He continued past the water cannons, followed by the two thousand marchers, each stepping over the hoses as if they were nothing, as if Billups were a modern-day Moses who had just parted the Red Sea.

Nonviolent resistance had done more here than merely expose hatred. It had disarmed hatred, transforming hate into compassion. One by one, the enemy was being won over.

By the end of May 6, another thousand people had been arrested, making this the largest number of nonviolent arrests in a single day in United States history. Twenty-five hundred young people were in custody. With no more prison space available, some children were relocated to fenced-in areas at the open-air fairgrounds, where it rained that evening.

May 7 was Operation Confusion. With the police unable to imprison any more protesters, three thousand activists marched wherever they liked in Birmingham, including the white commercial center. The campaign's nonviolent tactics had rendered the authorities largely powerless. As African American comedian Dick Gregory, who came to Birmingham to join Project C, put it, "Once you arrest three thousand people, you have no control, especially when they ain't scared of you."

White leaders in Birmingham reluctantly came to the conclusion that they had no choice but to negotiate with King and the rest of the movement leadership. A committee of whites and blacks, meeting into the early hours of May 8, attempted to reach an agreement. King called publicly on President Kennedy to "sign a paper saying that segregation is unconstitutional." Kennedy, though not yet ready to take such a bold step, held his first press conference in which race relations were the dominate subject.

Across the United States, all eyes were fixed on Birmingham.

On May 10 the terms of a settlement were finally

announced. Much like Gandhi before them, the movement leaders didn't get everything they wanted, but the compromise was meaningful nevertheless. Within ninety days: desegregation of lunch counters, restrooms, and the like. Within sixty days: At least one black would be hired at white-owned stores. And everyone in jail would be released on bond, using money collected primarily by large labor unions, like the United Auto Workers, across the country.

King called it a victory for democracy and for all of Birmingham, "white and black," again emphasizing that non-violent activism aims for justice and not the simple defeat of one's opponent. That day hundreds of children and teens, the heroes of Birmingham, were freed from jail and reunited with their proud, relieved families. With Project C having reached a successful conclusion, King left town and traveled to Atlanta.

But the long-standing scourge of racism and hatred hadn't simply been erased from Birmingham. So unpopular was the settlement among Birmingham's whites that only one white member of the committee was willing to be publicly identified.

Even worse, the next day another group held a rally just outside Birmingham to come up with their own response to the settlement: the Ku Klux Klan.

•

A little before 11:00 p.m. on May 11, a police car stopped at the home of A. D. King, a Birmingham minister and the younger brother of Martin Luther King Jr. The driver tossed an object in the direction of the house. Next a uniformed officer stepped from the car, ran toward the residence, and left a second object near the front steps. Moments later, after the car had sped off, the first object exploded, making an indentation in the ground a couple of feet in diameter.

Locals quickly gathered. Less than ten minutes later, the second item, filled with dynamite, detonated with a much larger explosion. It blew an eight-foot hole in the house's brick wall, blasted the front door into the kitchen, and shattered most every window. Miraculously, the Kings and their five children were not injured.

The crowd, now numbering more than a thousand, was already upset by the first blast. After the second, which was clearly timed to injure not just the Kings but those very bystanders, they were furious. The police arriving at the site of the attack were met by bricks, stones, and bottles.

A. D. King grabbed a police megaphone and preached nonviolence, but the situation was precarious.

Not an hour later a third explosion sounded, this one coming from downtown.

Wyatt Walker, who had meticulously planned Project C, was still in Birmingham, asked by Martin Luther King Jr. to stick around and tie up the campaign's loose ends. Walker hadn't seen his wife and children for nearly three months, so they were brought to Birmingham and put up at the Gaston Motel, the movement's temporary headquarters. Walker had rushed to A. D. King's house after the first two explosions. When he heard the third, he feared the worst.

"That's the motel," he said.

The building was miles away, but he was right.

The third bomb, thrown from the rear window of a Chevrolet that never even stopped, hit the motel directly under room 30, the suite where the movement leadership had met day after day for more than a month. The explosion blew a massive hole in the steel-reinforced concrete wall and destroyed a pair of trailers nearby.

The three bombs added up to two failed assassination attempts on the King brothers.

Twenty-five hundred Birmingham blacks gathered downtown late Saturday night, many of them coming straight from bars and pool halls. They were in no mood for another nonviolent demonstration.

"Eye for an eye, tooth for a tooth," one called out.

Storefronts near the Sixteenth Street Baptist Church were shattered. An Italian grocery store burst into flames, the fire soon leaping to two houses nearby. The police were showered with bricks and rocks. Fire trucks were prevented from reaching the blaze, which continued to spread along an entire city block. Car windows were smashed and stores were looted. A policeman was stabbed three times. Tear gas filled the air.

A. D. King, who left the destruction at his house to rush downtown, was leading the effort to bring the chaos under control. Through a megaphone he called out, "Our *home* was just bombed . . . If we who were in jeopardy of being killed, if we have gone away *not* angry, *not* throwing bricks . . . why must *you* rise up to hurt our cause? You are *hurting* us! You are *not* helping! Now won't you *please* clear this park."

By 2:30 a.m. the rioters were spent, but the night's conflict wasn't over. Just then, six hundred state troopers, led by Colonel Albert Lingo, appeared downtown, brandishing submachine guns and sawed-off shotguns.

Chief Jamie Moore of the Birmingham police eyed Lingo's arsenal and told him, "We don't need any guns down here. You all might get someone killed."

"You're damn right it'll kill somebody," Lingo answered.

Shouting to anyone still loitering to get inside, the troopers took to clearing the streets, violently. A *New York Times* reporter wrote that "the 'thonk' of clubs striking heads could be heard across the street."

Before dawn more than seventy people would be hospitalized.

Even Wyatt Walker himself came close to taking violent revenge that night. After returning to the Gaston Motel to check on his family, he learned that his wife, who had been unharmed by the bomb, had received a serious head injury from the butt of a state trooper's rifle. When the trooper in question was pointed out to Walker, he went to attack him, but was wrestled to the ground by a nearby reporter, probably saving Walker's life.

Miraculously, the settlement survived the violence of May 11. President Kennedy voiced his support for it on national television, and to ensure calm—along with sending a message to those state and local authorities still determined to maintain segregation—he ordered thousands of federal troops to the area.

The implementation of the agreement would be slow and frustratingly inconsistent. For instance, the white committee members would argue that they were only obligated to employ a single black employee in all the city's white stores. Nevertheless, the moderates, resigned to the eventual end of segregation, whatever the timetable, were now in charge. On May 23, Bull Connor was officially relieved of his duties.

Change would be slow and gradual in Birmingham. And violent racism wouldn't disappear all at once. Indeed, a few months later, on the morning of Sunday, September 15, a bomb planted by members of the Ku Klux Klan would devastate the Sixteenth Street Baptist Church, killing four girls inside.

Despite all this, Shuttlesworth's earlier claim—"as Birmingham goes, so goes the nation"—proved absolutely correct. The successful confrontation in this one city spread anti-segregation activism near and far. The summer of 1963 saw more than 750 nonviolent protests in nearly 200 cities, which led to the desegregation of more than 250 public places throughout the South.

Birmingham had not only emboldened grassroots activism across America's South, it had transformed the most powerful man in the country into an outspoken champion of civil rights. On the evening of June 11, President Kennedy took to the airwaves to address the nation, finally calling for equality among the races on moral grounds.

"I hope that every American, regardless of where he lives, will stop and examine his conscience," he began. Kennedy next reminded his audience of what they all knew. "This nation . . . was founded on the principle that all men are created equal." The president continued: "If an American, because his skin is dark, cannot eat lunch in a restaurant open to the public, if he cannot send his children to the best public school available, if he cannot vote for the public officials who will represent him, if, in short, he cannot enjoy the full and free life which all of us want, then who among us would be content to have the color of his skin changed and stand in his place?"

Echoing King's "Letter from a Birmingham Jail," Kennedy stated that "this nation, for all its hopes and all its boasts, will not be free until all its citizens are free."

The president ended his speech by turning from moral considerations to governmental measures. "Next week I shall ask the Congress of the United States to act, to make a commitment it has not fully made in this century to the proposition that race has no place in American life or law."

On August 28, a quarter of a million people participated in the March on Washington for Jobs and Freedom, a historic event organized by none other than Bayard Rustin. And it was here that King spoke his famous words: "I have a dream."

Moments before reaching that celebrated section of his speech, however, King reminded his audience of something else:

> We must forever conduct our struggle on the high plane of dignity and discipline. We must not allow our creative protest to degenerate into physical violence. Again and again, we must rise to the majestic heights of meeting physical force with soul force.

Though the reference was likely lost on many in attendance, King was alluding to Gandhi here, translating the Indian leader's satyagraha as "soul force." With these words, King was not just emphasizing the nonviolent philosophy at the center of the civil rights movement, he was declaring that his movement saw itself as the inheritor of Gandhi's teachings.

Because, as it turned out, Gandhi's methods *could* succeed in a different time and place. Better yet, the civil rights movement showed that through nonviolent activism, love could get the better of hate.

And as we'll see in the next chapter, nonviolent activism could craft a successful movement facing an even greater obstacle. Not that of hate, but of being a people ignored altogether, a people so powerless as to be utterly invisible.

A Nonviolent Dream. Martin Luther King Jr.'s famous speech at the March on Washington on August 28, 1963, reaffirmed his belief in the power of nonviolence.

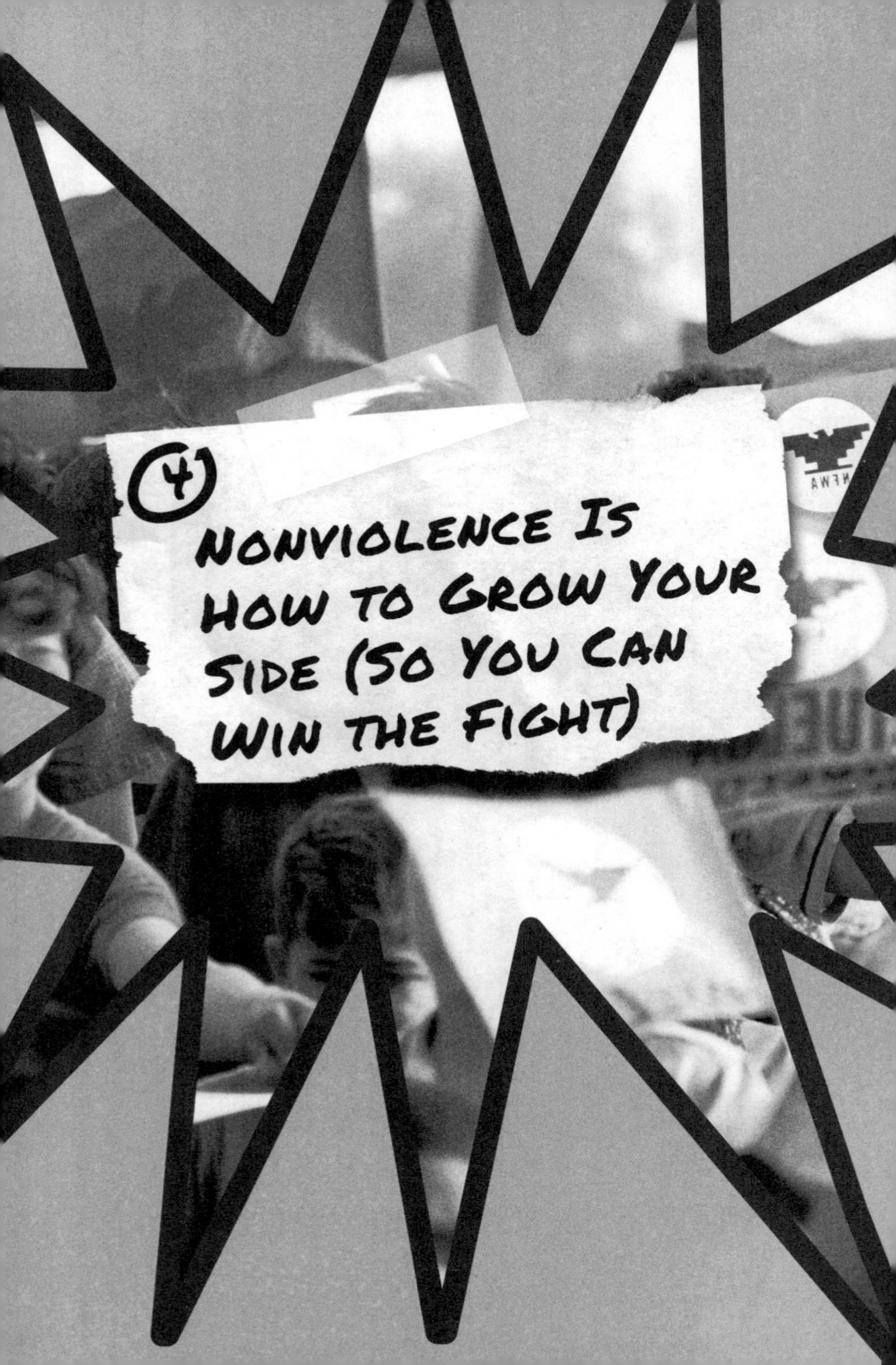

4 Nonviolence Is How to Grow Your Side (So You Can Win the Fight)

CESAR CHAVEZ and the FARMWORKERS MOVEMENT

Cesar Chavez, who led the farmworkers' fight for better working conditions, in 1966

"Once social change begins, it cannot be reversed. You cannot uneducate a person who has learned to read. You cannot humiliate the person who feels pride. You cannot oppress the people who are not afraid anymore."

—Cesar Chavez

AT FIRST THEY WERE NOTHING. THERE WERE HUNDREDS OF thousands of Mexican American farmworkers—many the children and grandchildren of immigrants brought legally to the United States in the first half of the twentieth century to work in California's ever-expanding fields—but together they were nothing.

Each morning they'd take their short-handled hoes, only eighteen inches long, and set out for the fields, where they'd work, bent over from dawn to dusk, until they couldn't stand up straight. When they got thirsty laboring in the hundred-degree heat, they'd drink filthy water from an irrigation ditch. When they had to go to the bathroom, they searched for some privacy, which in a wide-open field was often nowhere at all.

If they were lucky they'd get paid half the minimum wage, because farmworkers weren't protected under federal labor laws. The contractor who did the hiring might cheat them on their hours or tell them they hadn't worked hard enough. He'd pay them whatever he wanted, and there wasn't a thing they could do.

They couldn't just go home at the end of another long, backbreaking day in the fields either. Earning at most a few dollars for a dozen or more hours of work, they couldn't afford a permanent home. But even if they could, they wouldn't be able to stay there for long. These workers were migrants, following the crops and the growing seasons wherever they took them, up and down the giant state of California. Home was the road, or wherever they could find a place to sleep in the middle of a job. Under a bridge, on a riverbank, or in a dirty, crowded migrant camp, where the "houses" might be built from cardboard, where there was no electricity, where a single faucet had to be shared by hundreds of people.

Carrots in the winter only miles from the Mexican border, grapes farther north as spring approached, cherries an hour east of Los Angeles in May, apricots up near San Jose in the early summer, back down toward Fresno for cucumbers in August, and then south for cotton until the end of the year. Each job inflicted its own damage. Dry, cracked, calloused fingers; bent, crooked backs; and, thanks to potent pesticides, red eyes, itchy skin, and who knew what else in the places no one could see. And if a worker got hurt on the job, well, too bad.

Many workers didn't live to see fifty.

Maybe it would all be worth it if their children lived to see a better life. If the parents' sacrifice paid off in the end, if the American dream was available to these Mexican Americans, too. But how could a girl get a true education if she had to change schools every few months in order to follow her parents across the state? And what would a boy learn if he had to leave school forever at the age of twelve and head to the fields himself, because his parents, despite rarely taking a single day off, didn't earn enough to support their family? For farmworkers, life was a vicious cycle, the poverty handed down from generation to generation.

Most of them were too tired, too hungry, too poor, too busy, and too dejected searching for the next day's work to think about making things better. On those rare occasions when they tried, when they demanded better working conditions and higher wages, they were fired, or worse. The growers cared little about their workers, seeing them less as people than as "just another item in producing products, like fertilizer or boxes or water."

Even worse for the farmworkers, the growers had the politicians and the police on their side, and when that wasn't enough they had the money to pay enforcers ready to meet the farmworkers' demands with violence. Organizers went to jail, were beaten, or even killed.

So it's no wonder that a federal report in 1939 found "a shocking degree of human misery among farmworkers." But most Americans knew little about it. They went to their local supermarkets, bought grapes, watermelons, and lettuce, ignorant of the suffering that filled their shelves.

Most white Americans at least knew about the plight of African Americans. They knew about slavery, the Civil War, and the ongoing issue of segregation. Farmworkers didn't work in the homes of white Americans. They rarely lived in their communities, or even at the edges of them, and when they did, they faced their own WHITES ONLY signs. Many farmworkers didn't yet speak English very well, if at all, so how could they tell their story?

They were isolated. They were invisible. They were powerless.

There were hundreds of thousands of them, but together they were nothing.

•

Cesar Chavez was short, soft-spoken, and poorly educated. When he was born in Arizona in 1927, his family owned a store and some land. But they lost everything in the Great Depression. The rest of his childhood was spent migrating around California, his parents forever searching for farmwork. He attended thirty-seven different schools before hitting the fields for good when he still should have been in the seventh grade. His first job took him out to a cantaloupe field. They paid him eight cents an hour.

Chavez's mother, Juana Estrada, was illiterate but a very wise woman all the same. She often taught her son through dichos—or proverbs—many of which laid the groundwork for Cesar's devotion to nonviolence later in life. She encouraged him to "reject a culture which too often tells its young men that you're not a man if you don't fight back. She would say 'No, it's best to turn the other cheek. God gave you senses like a mind and tongue and you can get out of anything. It takes two to fight and one can't do it alone.'"

In truth, Chavez would become a fighter, and a leader of fighters as well, but his side would fight nonviolently.

By the age of twenty-five he was living with his

wife, Helen, in a bad part of San Jose populated by poor farmworkers called Sal Si Puedes, which means "get out if you can." In 1952 a man named Fred Ross came through town, representing the Community Service Organization (CSO). Ross was trying to convince Mexican Americans to band together and improve their situation.

Cesar Chavez avoided the persistent Ross for a while, annoyed by this white activist who thought he knew what people like Chavez needed. When he finally agreed to meet with Ross, Chavez brought along a bunch of thugs with him, intent on running Ross out of town. But the moment Ross opened his mouth, Chavez was hooked.

"Fred did such a good job of explaining how poor people could build power that I could even taste it. I could really feel it. I thought, gee, it's like digging a hole. There's nothing complicated about it."

Chavez joined Ross the very next night, going door-to-door to register voters. The new recruit amazed Ross with his curiosity, intelligence, and passion. "I think I've found the guy I'm looking for," Ross wrote in his diary. The CSO offered Chavez a job.

Chavez worked for the CSO for most of the next decade. A mediocre public speaker with sleepy eyes and no interest or ability in dressing nicely, Chavez didn't make much of a first impression with his people. But it hardly mattered; he was relentless, traveling around the state and urging his fellow Mexican Americans to learn about and demand their rights. Some had been in the United States for decades, but had never taken the necessary steps to become citizens. Others were citizens, but never registered to vote. If they could be convinced to claim their political voice, their impoverished, neglected communities would improve. The CSO would help them confront everything from "potholes to police brutality."

But not everyone welcomed Chavez and the work of the CSO. Local Republicans in San Jose were alarmed at the surge in Mexican Americans heading to the polls, since they tended to support Democratic candidates. When an effort to intimidate these new voters with illegal literacy tests failed, they accused Chavez of being a communist sympathizer. In addition to visits from the FBI, this smear lead to suspicion from his fellow Mexican American Catholics, for whom being a communist meant opposing religion altogether.

But these and other obstacles barely slowed Chavez down, and by 1958 he was CSO's national director. Only a few years later, however, Chavez decided to leave the organization. Despite everything that he and the CSO were doing to better Mexican American communities in their twenty-two offices around the state, he saw again and again that until the conditions for farmworkers improved, real change wouldn't come. Chavez knew they needed a union, one large and strong enough to force the growers to the bargaining table. But despite Chavez's pleas, the CSO wanted no part of such a daunting project. Many others had tried building a union before. Every last one of them had failed.

Chavez thought success was possible. Speaking of the growers, he said, "It's true, they're powerful all right," but that didn't mean they had *all* the power. He believed that the fate of the farmworkers lay in their own hands. "If the Movement fails," Chavez said, it will be because "the workers refuse to use their power to make it go."

But wait, what was their power? The farmworkers were dirt-poor and largely uneducated, so how could they influence all those people—the rich growers, the well-connected politicians, the armed police—who controlled their lives completely?

Chavez understood that the farmworkers had one thing those others groups lacked: numbers. There were hundreds of thousands of them. If they could come together, stick together, and act as one, they would have immense power.

And Chavez believed they could.

So he quit the best job he ever had and moved Helen and their eight children south to Delano, a quiet farm town in the San Joaquin Valley with a population of twelve thousand. He and Helen had family there who could help support them while he set out to organize all their many people.

The Chavez family would need this help, because Cesar was taking on the monumental task of making something out of nothing.

All while unemployed.

Thankfully, Chavez wasn't working alone. Not even at the very beginning. Armed with little more than his steadfast conviction, he managed to recruit those closest to him, prying them away from their current careers and plans for the future.

In addition to Helen—who raised their kids, returned to the fields to make money, and helped however else she could—there was Richard Chavez, Cesar's younger brother and closest friend since childhood. Richard was working as a carpenter in Delano when Cesar arrived. A bit of a softie, he couldn't say no to his big brother. Soon he was on board.

Manuel Chavez, Cesar's slick, sweet-talking cousin, had escaped the fields and was making good money selling used cars in San Diego. He returned to Delano reluctantly and, he claimed, only for a little while. "If in six months we don't organize farm workers, I'm going to leave you," he told Cesar. Manuel never sold another car again.

It wasn't all kept in the family. Julio Hernandez joined after Cesar and Manuel, having not eaten for a couple days while on the road meeting with farmworkers, knocked on Julio's door to ask for food. Hernandez was skeptical, having been burned by previous failed efforts at unionizing, but he turned out to be an outstanding recruiter. "The harder a guy is to convince, the better leader or member he becomes," Chavez said.

Chavez had recruited the gifted organizer Gilbert Padilla to the CSO in 1956; Padilla, or Flaco (Skinny) as they called him, didn't leave the CSO right away after Chavez relocated to Delano, but he came down whenever he could, taking on extra hours in the fields, where he could reach farmworkers directly. By the end of 1962, he was working with Chavez full-time.

Most important was the brilliant, tough Dolores

Huerta. Other than Cesar, no one would contribute more to the movement than she. Discovered by Fred Ross and brought into the CSO back in 1955, she stayed on for a while at the organization's Stockton office after Chavez left. But she longed for a union and devoted every spare moment to the new organizing efforts. Along with Helen and Cesar, Huerta helped name the group they were building: the Farm Workers Association (FWA). She also sat over a map with the two of them and divided up all the relevant farm towns and labor camps scattered across the state.

Because that was the main work to be done at this early stage: visit each place their fellow workers lived. And once they got there, what would they do? Register every last farmworker they could find.

They printed four-by-six-inch registration cards in an effort to collect simple information. Name, birth date, stuff like that. And an answer to a crucial question: How much should our minimum wage be? Nothing complicated, nothing glamorous. It was as simple as organizing can get.

But when a brand-new organization has no money, affording even basic supplies can be a challenge. Fortunately, in order to print all those cards, the FWA got an old mimeograph machine (they set it up in

Richard's garage) from a group called the California Migrant Ministry (CMM).

Chris Hartmire, who grew up an affluent white kid in Philadelphia, was the head of the CMM, a church group that provided charity for farmworkers. Hartmire believed in their work, but it wasn't until he crossed paths with Chavez that he figured out how best to help. When Chavez met with CMM's pastors, Hartmire was awed by the activist's ability to take charge. "He was organizing us," Hartmire said. This was Chavez's genius in action, a knack not just for mobilizing his own people, but for creating alliances, for getting other people to join his side in the struggle.

Hartmire soon threw CMM's financial resources behind the effort, and assigned the Reverend Jim Drake to work right alongside Chavez.

Over the course of six months in the middle of 1962 and with the support of his inner circle, Chavez drove his 1953 Mercury station wagon thousands of miles all over the valley, putting in sixteen-hour days, setting up local committees, telling any worker who would listen about the new association, and encouraging everyone to fill out those registration cards.

One name at a time, the movement grew.

•

On September 30, 1962, 150 delegates and their families assembled in an abandoned theater in Fresno for the founding convention of the National Farm Workers Association (NFWA). After Huerta led everyone in the Pledge of Allegiance, Chavez shared the promising news that twenty-five thousand registration cards had already been filled out. The delegates called for a farmworker minimum wage of $1.50 (the equivalent of around $12.50 in 2020) and agreed to monthly dues in order to support the ongoing registration effort and provide life insurance for its members.

The old theater still held a big screen at its front. When the gathering began, it was covered in paper. Late in the meeting, at Chavez's signal, Manuel pulled a cord, the paper tore away, revealing underneath the association's new flag: a black eagle on a white circle against a red background. The crowd gasped at the sight of this bold, powerful image. When asked to explain the design, Manuel, always fast on his feet, improvised a fitting answer: "Black was for the workers' desperation, white was for their hope, and red was for their sacrifice." Simple to reproduce, it was an emblem most anyone could share.

The farmworkers had a name—NFWA—and a flag to represent them. They had an identity. They were no longer nothing.

In time the eagle would fly far and wide, but for now it still kept a low profile. After all, they were calling themselves only an association and not a union, even though that's what everyone ultimately wanted. But when people heard "union" they heard "strike," and no one, least of all Chavez, wanted that quite yet. Their side still wasn't big or strong enough for such a fight.

Which isn't to say that when the first strike came they felt all that ready.

Three years later, on September 16, 1965, Mexican Independence Day, Chavez rose to speak before a lively crowd of some fifteen hundred people who packed Delano's Our Lady of Guadalupe Church.

> You are here to discuss a matter which is of extreme importance to yourselves, your families and all the community . . . One hundred and fifty-five years ago in the state of Guanajuato in Mexico, a padre proclaimed the struggle for liberty. He was killed, but ten years later Mexico

> won its independence. We are engaged in another struggle for freedom and dignity which poverty denies us.

Chavez convened this general meeting to get approval to call a strike. But the boisterous crowd's chant, which reached all the way up to the packed balcony on the second floor, of "Huelga, huelga, huelga!"—"Strike, strike, strike!"—made it clear that the coming vote was just a formality.

Still, Chavez worried that this strike was premature.

That year's grape harvest, which began south of Delano in the Coachella Valley, brought conflict. Growers, claiming they needed extra workers in order to pick all their grapes before they rotted on the vine, convinced the government to reinstate the bracero program, which had been outlawed in 1964. Braceros were temporary guest workers brought in from Mexico. By using them, the already powerful growers could lower wages and punish local workers who caused trouble, simply by not hiring them. It was another unfair feature of an unjust system, and its end had been celebrated by domestic farmworkers everywhere.

But now the braceros were returning. Even worse, the Coachella growers paid these guest workers fifteen cents more an hour than the Filipino American workers in the valley normally received. So those workers went on strike, and ten days later their pay was raised. By early September, the grape harvest had moved north, reaching Delano, where the growers were offering domestic laborers a measly two-thirds of the braceros' hourly wage. The Filipino workers, many of whom had migrated from Coachella to Delano along with the harvest, went on strike in nine vineyards. And this time they and their leader, Larry Itliong, were asking Chavez and the NFWA to join them.

Chavez knew they had no choice. If the NFWA didn't join the strike, they'd be hanging their fellow Filipino workers out to dry and helping the greedy growers in the process. Everyone in the church agreed and the vote to strike was unanimous. But this wasn't just another decision; it would be the pivotal moment in the NFWA's short history. Chavez was far from certain they were up for it. "Oh God," he would recall thinking some months later, "we're not ready for a strike."

Since the founding convention almost three years earlier, Chavez and his team had continued registering and recruiting. They founded a much-loved newspaper, *El Malcriado* (the Unruly One), which gave farmworkers a voice, told their stories, and kept them informed, strengthening their group identity much like the eagle had before. With each new recruit, the NFWA was increasing a force that, one day, could confront the growers head-on.

But Chavez worried that it was too soon for the NFWA to move from organizing to action. They had over a thousand members, but fewer than 20 percent of those were actually paying dues. To execute a successful strike, the farmworkers' only hope was having not just greater numbers, but dedicated, devoted, well-organized numbers, an army of farmworkers ready and able to sacrifice for their side.

Despite his doubts, Chavez prepared his troops for the battle ahead. He knew it wasn't enough to inspire them to join the next stage of this conflict; he now had to teach them *how* to fight as well: "But it must not be a violent struggle," he told the crowd, "even if violence is used against us. Violence can only hurt us and our cause."

Chavez's formal education wasn't much, so he had to teach himself. Once he discovered Gandhi, whose philosophy echoed strongly with the proverbs his mother had taught him as a child, Chavez became a devoted student of nonviolent history and strategy. He read about the great Indian leader and closely followed the American civil rights movement, which was still ongoing. He acquired a deep understanding of how nonviolent struggle works and envisioned the union as a "nonviolent army" of incredible strength.

But was his army ready to battle?

They were about to find out.

Before calling the meeting to a close, Chavez once again implored them to strike nonviolently.

"Are you in agreement?"

"Sí!"

Near the end of the church meeting, the workers were asked to fill out authorization cards giving the NFWA permission to represent them. Over the next few days, twenty-seven hundred cards poured in. This was an impressive number, and a great sign, since it meant that those who attended the meeting were enthusiastic enough to go out and recruit many others who weren't there. The threat of a strike wasn't driving people away, just the opposite.

All the same, Chavez still hoped to avert a strike. He and his leadership reached out to local growers however they could, hoping both sides could sit down and hash out their differences. Phone calls were made, letters were sent, they even convinced the mayor of Delano to ask the growers to come to city hall and negotiate. But the growers ignored them entirely. After all, why negotiate with people you control completely?

And Chavez was right to be worried about the challenge of a strike, especially one targeting farms. The organizers and their pickets had to cover four hundred square miles stretching across forty-eight different ranches, each with dozens of entrances. Many workers still didn't know about the strike, while some knew but didn't want any part of it. To make matters worse, growers brought in scabs, workers from elsewhere willing to cross the picket lines.

Armed with HUELGA signs and megaphones, the union members scattered out as best they could, pleading with those heading out into the vineyards not to betray their fellow workers and join the strike instead.

With the growers and their henchmen not taking kindly to the strike, it didn't take long for each and every farmworker to see there would be no neutral ground in this battle. Foremen hopped into tractors and drove back and forth by the picketers, covering them in dust. Others preferred their pickup trucks, which lifted less dirt into the air, but which could be driven at high speeds dangerously close to the defenseless strikers. More than a few ankles were nipped. When these tactics didn't work, the growers' men seized the strikers' picket signs and lit them on fire. Next they assaulted the strikers themselves, cursing at them, beating them, turning their dogs on them, spraying them with sulfur pesticides, or simply pointing their shotguns right in their faces and threatening their lives.

How did the police respond? Mostly by trailing the union organizers as they drove from field to field, jotting down license plate numbers and photographing strikers for their records. And sometimes they'd arrest someone calling out, "Huelga!"

For disturbing the peace.

But all this ruthless, violent intimidation turned the fields into the union's most fertile recruiting grounds yet. Watching union members courageously endure these cruel efforts to crush the strike inspired many farmworkers to join them. Laborers would drop their tools right there in the field, walk down the row, step out onto the roadside, pick up a sign, and join the strike.

The strength of nonviolent sacrifice was infectious.

Chavez knew this struggle would be long and hard, but he believed their strategy would prevail. "If we can keep our great strike peaceful, nonviolent, and strong, we cannot lose." Why was he so sure? Because, as he put it, "They have the money and the power, but there are thousands of us and very few of them."

•

After a few weeks of this, the exasperated sheriff of Kern County, Roy Galyen, declared that shouting the word "huelga" would now be illegal. In response, on October 19, a number of strikers, including Helen Chavez and some clergy, gathered at the W. B. Camp Ranch on the outskirts of Delano and raised their voices together:

"Huelga! Huelga! Huelga!"

Forty-four were arrested.

The timing was perfect. Cesar Chavez was heading north that same day, to speak about the strike at the University of California, Berkeley. Five hundred students, supporters of the civil rights and free speech movements, responded to Chavez's announcement of the arrests with their own chant of "Huelga! Huelga! Huelga!" More than this, they dug into their pockets to support the strike. Chavez's tour of the Bay Area included visits to Stanford University, Mills College, and San Francisco State University. He returned to Delano with $6,700—more than $50,000 in today's dollars.

Many in those college audiences were inspired to give more than money. This was the mid-1960s, activism was in the air, and with it a belief that you could make the world a more just place. Soon young students were the ones migrating, trekking down to Delano to strengthen the strike however they could, collecting food and money, joining the pickets, and spending each night on someone's floor in a sleeping bag. Some stayed for a weekend, while some completely left behind their lives in the city and stayed on for years.

They weren't the only allies chipping in. Day by day, the number of clergy openly supporting the union grew, and their backing gave the movement a legitimacy many so-called radical movements lack. Chavez's people were also contacted by the San Francisco branch of the Student Nonviolent Coordinating Committee (SNCC), one of the key organizations of the civil rights movement. Soon SNCC volunteers were coming down and offering workshops in nonviolence.

At its core, this was a showdown between farmworkers and growers. If you weren't in one of these two groups—and 200 million Americans across the country were not—then technically you stood on the sidelines of this battle. But Chavez and the NFWA had figured something out: If they could convince these bystanders to join their side in the struggle, they'd be unstoppable.

Meanwhile, the press was finally getting wind of the conflict in the fields. For the very first time, national papers like the *New York Times* and the *Chicago Tribune*, intrigued by these arrests, ran stories on the strike. The drama of nonviolent resistance was a story they could sell to their readers, a story in which the heroes and villains weren't hard to tell apart.

As Chavez put it, explaining political jiujitsu in his own words, "We took every case of violence and publicized what they were doing to us. By some strange chemistry, every time the opposition commits an unjust act against our hopes and aspirations, we get tenfold paid back in benefits."

Despite all these promising signs, the first year of the strike had limited effect. It was simply too easy for the growers to locate scabs willing to replace the strikers. Many union members, needing to feed their families, left Delano for work elsewhere or reluctantly put down their signs and returned to the fields in town. The union solicited donations for food and money to keep the strikers and their children from starving, but all the same, the numbers on the picket line kept shrinking.

The year 1965 would bring a record crop.

Even worse, the grape harvest was reaching its end. Soon the November rains would begin, and then there would be no work in the vineyards until January.

What's a striker to do when there's nothing left to strike against?

•

Contemplating next steps, the strikers asked themselves a simple question: Where do all those grapes go once they leave the vineyards? A few of them decided to follow trucks packed with grapes up to San Francisco, hoping to make a scene wherever they were unloaded. They soon found themselves at the city's Pier 50. These grapes were headed to Japan aboard the SS *President Wilson.*

Gilbert Padilla walked out onto the pier with a homemade cardboard sign that read DON'T EAT GRAPES.

One of the longshoremen approached him. "Is this a labor dispute?" the man asked.

A little nervous, Padilla answered no.

A bit later a man named Jimmy Herman asked Padilla what exactly he was doing there. Once Padilla started to explain, Herman said, "Come with me." So he followed Herman, who just so happened to be the president of his local longshoremen's union, to his office. Padilla tells the rest of the story:

> He got on his hands and knees, Jimmy Herman, and he made picket signs. And he told me 'You go back there and don't tell nobody about who gave you this. But you just stand there' . . . The sign said,

> 'Farm Workers on Strike.' And everybody walked out . . . I felt like I was ten feet tall.

The docks at Pier 50 shut down. Clerks, longshoremen, and drivers all stopped working. Trucks backed up for miles. Fifty longshoremen even joined the pickets themselves. Twelve hundred and fifty cases of grapes sat on the dock for days, slowly rotting, until they were moved to cold storage. This technique was repeated successfully at a dock across the bay in Oakland as well.

The rural NFWA had found an additional set of allies, the organized labor of urban unions, to add to the clergy and college students already on their side. Unfortunately, the growers brought a lawsuit against the longshoremen, claiming that their participation in such "secondary boycotts," like the one that took place on Pier 50, was illegal. The courts ruled in the growers' favor and, just like that, the docks were up and running again.

But this was just a temporary setback, because the NFWA now had the answer for what to do while the fields sat silent down in Delano.

Instead of targeting production by striking, they'd fix their sights on consumption with a boycott. If they couldn't keep grapes from being harvested, if they couldn't keep them off the trucks and ships that took them to stores, they'd find ways to discourage regular consumers from buying them at their local supermarket.

Because growers don't just need to grow and harvest grapes, they need to sell them, too.

While the winter rains fell and the first wave of volunteers were sent to major cities across the country to begin organizing the boycott, Chavez searched for ways to strengthen the cause among those still in Delano. An avid student of nonviolent activism, Chavez knew there were more tactics available to them than just striking and boycotting. So he looked for an action that would both fortify the movement for the long struggle ahead—a wide-scale boycott was a huge undertaking—as well as draw attention to the cause from far and wide.

Thinking back to Gandhi while taking note of recent events in the American South—where civil rights activists, withstanding brutal police violence, walked the fifty-four miles between Selma, Mississippi, and Montgomery, Alabama, to demand voting rights—he found the answer: a march.

Three hundred miles separated Delano from Sacramento, the state's capital, which would be their destination. A long march to be sure, but one that could provide ample opportunities for publicity along

One Step at a Time. The farmworkers' march from Delano to Sacramento took the showdown from the fields to the state capital.

the way. Even better, the path between the two cities snaked through dozens of farm towns, where many farmworkers still knew little about the cause.

Like Gandhi, Paul, and King before him, Chavez based his belief in nonviolence on his religion, in this case Catholicism. So, it wouldn't just be a march, it

would be a peregrinación, a pilgrimage. They would head out in the month of March, during Lent, and reach the capital on Easter Sunday. The pilgrimage to Sacramento would be an extended penance, an act of purification. The marchers would choose to endure sacrifice and suffering in order to steel themselves and build solidarity for the future hardships their nonviolent activism would demand of them.

The pilgrimage commenced on the morning of March 17, 1966. Around one hundred marchers were still heading down Garces Highway in Delano when they were met by the police, intent on preventing them from moving through town without a parade permit. Thirty officers, arms locked together, confronted the marchers, who came to a stop right in front of them. Some of the marchers went down on their knees and prayed.

Chavez approached them. “We’ll stay here if it takes a year, but we’re going to march through the city.”

After three hours the police chief relented, and the march continued.

Much like the Salt March some thirty-six years earlier, the peregrinación held programs each evening in a different town, where dramatic readings would educate listeners about the union and recruit new members:

> We are tired of words, of betrayals, of indifference. *We shall be heard* . . . We are not afraid to suffer in order to win our cause . . . Our revolution will not be armed, but we want the existing social order to dissolve . . . Our

pilgrimage is the match that will light our cause for all farmworkers to see what is happening here, so that they may do as we have done.

Each morning the number of those marching behind a banner bearing the likeness of la Virgen de Guadalupe would increase, along with the fervor of the marchers themselves.

And the marchers would need this inspiration, as all those steps took a toll. Chavez suffered perhaps the most. With no time or inclination to secure proper hiking boots for himself before setting out, he marched in "worn-out low shoes." The first day wasn't even over when his ankle swelled up "like a melon" and the sole of his "left foot was just one huge blister." But because this was a penitential march, he refused to take painkillers. He only made it through the rest of the pilgrimage with the help of a cane.

Chavez was hardly the only one who paid a physical price. As Angie Hernandez, the daughter of Julio, put it, "Some people had bloody feet, some would keep on walking and you'd see blood coming out of their shoes." Of course, such pain, including injuries much worse than bloody feet, was familiar to the farmworkers from their long days in the fields. The difference this time around? They were choosing the hardship. They took ownership of their suffering with each painful step and demonstrated the strength to endure it for their cause.

The growers watched all this "with a mixture of bafflement, anger, and apprehension." But they were still convinced that their power would once more overwhelm the farmworkers, to the point that they refused to acknowledge they were in the middle of a labor dispute at all. On March 24, grower Martin Zaninovich, altogether ignoring the march and the boycott as well, said, "The simple truth is that there is no strike in Delano."

The number of marchers and the size of the welcoming crowds grew with each town they reached. These towns often fed the marchers dinner upon their arrival and breakfast before they left the next morning. In between, many residents opened their modest homes to provide shelter for the weary travelers, though at times their numbers were too great, leaving some with no choice but to spend the night camped out on a friendly stranger's lawn.

On April 10, Easter Sunday, the marchers crossed a bridge leading to the state's capital, where they were met by ten thousand supporters. A three-hour rally to celebrate the longest protest march in U.S. history was held, the fifty-seven original marchers honored on the stage. Dolores Huerta spoke to the vast crowd, calling out a key resident of Sacramento who elected to leave town rather than meet with the marchers: Governor Pat Brown. She demanded that he

> call a special session of the legislature to enact a collective bargaining law for the state of California. We will be satisfied with nothing less . . . You cannot close your eyes and your ears to us any longer. You cannot pretend we do not exist. You cannot plead ignorance to our problems because we are here . . . And we are not alone.

At first, the union announced a boycott of just one company, Schenley Industries. Schenley only had a small vineyard in the Delano area, but the fact that it made most of its money selling well-known brands of alcohol, like Cutty Sark and Dewar's, made it a convenient target. It didn't matter that these products weren't actually made of grapes themselves; they were recognizable and thus easy to single out. Before the march to Sacramento was even over, Schenley agreed to negotiate a contract rather than face a costly boycott.

After Schenley came DiGiorgio Fruit Corporation, a

much more formidable opponent. No one in the country grew more grapes than DiGiorgio. Not only that, the company had a long history of dealing ruthlessly with unions and their strikers. But like Schenley, DiGiorgio sold its own line of products in stores with names like S&W Fine Foods and TreeSweet Companies. Once again, these products, and not grapes themselves, would be the target of a boycott.

The battle with DiGiorgio would prove tougher than the one with Schenley. DiGiorgio expressed a willingness to negotiate with the union, but only if it could prove that it truly represented the workers. This meant an election. Farmworkers would vote to decide if they wanted to be represented by the NFWA, the union Chavez led, or by no union at all. If a majority of farmworkers didn't choose the NFWA, the union would have no leg to stand on, boycott or no boycott.

Early in the run-up to the election another adversary appeared: the Teamsters. They were a well-established, but terribly corrupt, union, one whose leadership was known for its ties to organized crime and its practice of cutting backroom deals with management. Their operatives, brought in by DiGiorgio, were now registering farmworkers in the fields as well, giving voters a third choice in the elections. The fight was now two against one, and the two had way more resources on their side.

Not satisfied with their obvious advantages, DiGiorgio also began firing workers who openly supported the NFWA. There was talk that fired workers might be declared eligible to vote, but these were migrant workers who could well be halfway across the state, bent over in someone else's fields, by the time election day came.

On June 21, while the two sides were still discussing the exact rules of the election, DiGiorgio suddenly announced that voting would take place in only three days' time. DiGiorgio would print the ballots, and the election would be overseen by a private firm of their choosing, and not by government representatives, which was standard practice. Chavez called for a boycott of the election itself, which, to no one's surprise, the Teamsters won.

DiGiorgio had successfully rigged the election, and it seemed that all might be lost. But at a convention just a few days later, Chavez and Dolores Huerta publicly confronted California Governor Pat Brown, who was running for reelection himself. They made it clear to him if he didn't do something about this rigged election, he would lose the support of not just the NFWA, but of its allies as well, which included the mighty AFL-CIO, the largest federation of unions in the country.

Brown had no choice but to call for an investigation. Once its findings were delivered, new elections were approved. This time around, and in the face of escalating intimidation and violence from the Teamsters, the NWFA doubled its efforts, going so far as to bring a busload of recently fired workers from Texas back to California to vote.

On the evening of August 30, the union congregated in Filipino Hall in Delano, anxious for the results. A worried Chavez was busy "making plans for what to do in case we lost." Huerta called in from San Francisco, where the votes had been tallied. The NFWA had claimed more than 60 percent of the votes. "Everyone just exploded," said Eliseo Medina, an organizer who required ten stitches after being roughed up by the Teamsters during the campaign. "People were jumping up and hugging. It was such a feeling of euphoria and happiness."

Satisfaction with these results wasn't limited to farmworkers in California. Just a few weeks later, Chavez received a telegram from the other side of the country. It read "I extend the hand of fellowship and good will and wish continuing success to you and your members.

The fight for equality must be fought on many fronts."

The author of this message? Martin Luther King Jr.

The union, which soon switched its name to United Farm Workers (UFW), was making progress, but it was awfully slow. Even after these hard-fought victories, only one out of every fifty farmworkers was covered under the new contracts. Even worse, DiGiorgio discovered a counter-tactic of their own that other companies were sure to use: they simply switched the labels on their products, making it impossible for any shopper to know which companies they were actually supporting with their purchases.

It was now 1967, and the union had moved on to the Giumarra Companies, which grew more grapes in the San Joaquin Valley than anyone else, including DiGiorgio. As Dolores Huerta put it, "If we can crack Giumarra, we can crack them all." And this time actual grapes would be part of the boycott.

Fifty boycotters were sent on a school bus to New York, with the aim of preventing Giumarra grapes from reaching stores by converting distributors to the union's side. But how exactly would they do that? As Chavez spoke to them in the Delano headquarters before they headed out, he had to admit he didn't really know. They would have to produce results through sheer, unrelenting effort, working "single-mindedly, day and night."

The fifty were told: "Do not even entertain the idea of failure." Chavez, always one to lead by example, put the matter plainly to them: "He told them they were fanatics, just like him."

The year 1967 gave way to 1968. The boycotters in New York worked as Chavez instructed them and won over many sympathizers, including John Lindsay, the mayor of New York.

But Giumarra had borrowed the DiGiorgio trick and was using more than a hundred different labels to disguise their grapes, rendering the boycott toothless.

A radical idea, first floated by Delores Huerta and Fred Ross, was adopted. Chavez appeared on the *TODAY* show and made his boldest announcement yet: the boycott would be extended to all grapes across North America. If the growers were determined to make it impossible to tell them apart, the union would treat them all as one.

Chavez's message to viewers at home across the country couldn't have been simpler: "Don't eat grapes."

•

A second decision was made as well: the union's most dedicated and effective members would fight on the boycott's front lines. This meant sending activists and organizers, who had been busy striking and recruiting in the Valley for over two years, to cities all across North America. These farmworkers were to replace college students as the face of the boycott. Consumers would now see, as they were approached in supermarket parking lots, the actual human beings affected by the decisions they made as they wheeled their shopping carts to the checkout line.

The message would be straightforward enough for anyone to understand: "Please don't shop at this store so that farmworkers can earn a decent living and have toilets and water in the fields."

They were Mexican American farmworkers, many of whom knew little or no English. They had no savings. They had spent most of their lives in rural California. They had no idea where they'd stay in the cities they were assigned to, nor what to do for money once they got there. The union didn't have many resources to give them; they'd all be paid only five dollars a week. And there was no money to run any kind of advertising campaign. They'd have to spread the word and raise awareness all by themselves.

•

When Eliseo Medina was told he was being sent to Chicago, the twenty-one-year-old who had never left Delano wanted to know: "Where's Chicago?"

He figured it was an hour away by car.

Medina was given a one-way ticket to get on an airplane for the first time in his life, twenty bucks, a bag of UFW buttons, and the name of a mailman in Chicago who supported the union. When he arrived in the Windy City, Medina looked up the number of a local A&P supermarket and gave them a call.

"Hi, I'm a farmworker and I'd like you to stop selling grapes," he said.

Al and Elena Rojas put their three children in a Volkswagen and drove them to Pittsburgh to organize the boycott there. Just before leaving, Chavez came to say goodbye. Rojas thought to himself, "This is my chance to ask him the real big question . . . 'Cesar,' I said, 'How do you do a boycott?'"

Chavez didn't pretend to know. "To be truthful . . . I don't know how you do a boycott. You just go out there and tell those people to stop eating grapes. Get them to stop eating grapes."

And Rojas would spend more than two years in a strange city doing just that.

•

Jessica Govea was sent to Canada. Though a onetime farmworker herself, Govea was better educated than most of the other boycotters and was actually in college when she elected to drop out and join the fight. But after making some headway in Toronto, she was moved to mostly French-speaking Montreal. Sleeping on floors she would often cry herself to sleep from loneliness, and when the money got low, she subsisted on candy bars.

The growers looked for ways to fight back. They appealed to the new Republican governor and future president, Ronald Reagan, to intervene. Reagan was a friend of big business and thought the boycott was immoral. He reached out to the Teamsters to support the growers, and asked his secretary of agriculture, J. Earl Coke, to see what he could do to stop it.

When little came from this strategy, the growers hired a public relations firm with the aim of convincing people that they weren't the villains in this fight. Growers also filed lawsuits, hoping to have the boycott declared illegal altogether. They even tried to appeal to the supermarkets directly. A group of growers traveled to almost seventy locations around North America, warning executives that they'd find themselves powerless if they gave into the boycotters' demands.

Don't Buy Grapes. Jessica Govea (in glasses) was sent to Toronto, where she expanded the boycott through a variety of methods, including protest marches.

Finally, the growers smeared Chavez himself. John Giumarra Jr. told one supermarket association that Chavez was a threat to the very structure of American democracy. "You can't do business with Cesar Chavez," he said, "any more than you could do business with Hitler."

Despite all these efforts, the growers were no longer the ones with the power to shape the outcome of the boycott. North American consumers would determine this battle's winner, because the farmworkers' real opposition was the indifference of the average American. If the organizers of the boycott couldn't get the folks pushing their carts through the supermarket aisles to start caring about their struggle, nothing would change; the growers would remain on top.

So the boycotters and their increasingly active allies did whatever they could to draw attention to the cause, all with the hopes of convincing consumers to join their side. Pickets, speeches, marches, leaflets, sit-ins, candlelight vigils, and skits were just the beginning, as activists drew creatively from an ever-growing list of nonviolent tactics and strategies:

> Priests sat in produce aisles and prayed over grapes . . . Supporters bought shares in Safeway and Jewel supermarkets and disrupted annual meetings. Boycotters stalled cars to block supermarket parking lot entrances. Shoppers loaded carts with frozen goods on the bottom, piles of cans on top, and then asked at the checkout counter whether the store carried grapes. Receiving the affirmative answer they expected, they abandoned their carts in protest.

And, of course, they spoke to average Americans who had come to buy their groceries. One by one, these shoppers heard the activists' stories and came to understand that they were doing more than simply crossing another item off their list when they grabbed a bag of grapes. They were supporting growers who underpaid, mistreated, and refused to bargain collectively with their workers.

One by one, millions of North Americans, from Los Angeles to Montreal, came to understand that shopping for grapes was more than an errand, it was a moral issue. Americans learned that they could make a difference even if they lived thousands of miles away from the fields. And their decision *would* make a difference: either they would buy grapes and support the growers and the current system that favored them, or they would join the boycott and help bring about change.

As Jessica Govea told these customers, "What we're asking you to do is to become involved in our struggle and to help us by not buying grapes."

And, it turned out, plenty of shoppers were willing to get involved, by giving up grapes and choosing sides in this battle they, until recently, knew nothing about. Sales began to drop. Between 1966 and 1969, sales fell by 34 percent in New York, 41 percent in Chicago, and 42 percent in Boston. In Baltimore they fell by more than half.

And many shoppers weren't just refusing to buy grapes; they were refusing to enter stores that sold them.

Supermarkets sell thousands of different items, with grapes being just one. If carrying them meant protests, bad publicity, in-store confrontations, and fewer customers, then maybe their shelves would be more inviting without them at all. These stores, themselves owned by massive, powerful corporations, were a link in a long chain connecting them to growers, but now they, too, were coming over to the union's side. Address your labor issues, they told companies like Giumarra, or we won't carry your grapes.

As Medina put it, "We just totally disrupted all of these stores and we were a pain. I mean, we were terrible. We made life miserable for the stores and so they finally figured out we were more trouble than the grapes were worth . . . We got every single chain store in Chicago to stop selling grapes."

Chicago wasn't the only place where the boycotts were having a major effect. By Independence Day 1969, California grapes were no longer being sold in Detroit, New York, Boston, Philadelphia, Montreal, and Toronto. Growers couldn't find a destination for more than one out of every five grapes harvested that year. As a result,

"Millions of pounds of grapes were rotting in storage sheds."

The grape boycott, led by Mexican American farmworkers and their allies, would become "the biggest, most successful boycott in U.S. history." Seventeen mil-

A Just Contract. After five years of organizing, striking, marching, and boycotting, the growers and the farmworkers at last came together under terms acceptable to both sides.

lion Americans joined the side of the farmworkers and stopped buying grapes.

On July 29, 1970, the back doors of Reuther Hall at UFW headquarters in Delano opened and representatives from twenty-nine growers, including Giumarra, entered. Hundreds of jubilant farmworkers were waiting for them inside. The growers approached a long table, where Chavez sat, "wearing an immaculate, white high-collared Filipino dress shirt," which was about as dressed up as he'd ever get.

Because today was a special occasion. The growers had come to sign contracts.

John Giumarra Jr. signed his contract and raised his hands in the air, as if he were at long last surrendering to his stronger opponent. But his words suggested something else, a hope that now there would no longer be two sides at all: "If it works well here, if this experiment in social justice, as they call it, if it works here it can work elsewhere. But if it doesn't work here it won't work anywhere."

Farmworkers would now earn at least $1.80 an hour, more than $11 an hour in today's money. Employers would pay an additional ten cents into a health plan for every hour worked. Growers would also have to provide fresh drinking water, toilets out in the fields, and regular periods for rest.

Grapes grown and harvested by workers with these contracts would be sold with the union label on the package, a label proudly displaying the black eagle first unveiled almost eight years earlier.

The growers and the farmworkers were now partners in perhaps the most vital, most fundamental task of all: feeding millions and millions of people. Though there would be many more battles ahead, involving other crops and other farming communities, when it came to grapes, a nonviolent struggle had replaced injustice with justice, and in doing so had put everyone on the same side.

Chavez, who had led a movement that achieved what no one said could be done, spoke last: "Without the help of those millions upon millions of people who believe as we do that nonviolence is the way to struggle . . . I'm sure that we wouldn't be here today."

Chavez understood that the union won because they grew their movement day after day, year after year, until it was too big to be stopped. Most of these people joined the struggle not because they already believed in nonviolence, but because nonviolence showed them that this was a struggle worth joining.

The Eagle Flies. Richard Chavez, Cesar's brother, proudly displays a new crate of "union" grapes in 1970.

Nonviolent activism had transformed nothing into something, and into something mighty at that. But could nonviolence succeed in a closed society, where human rights didn't matter, where an undemocratic government controlled daily life in every way?

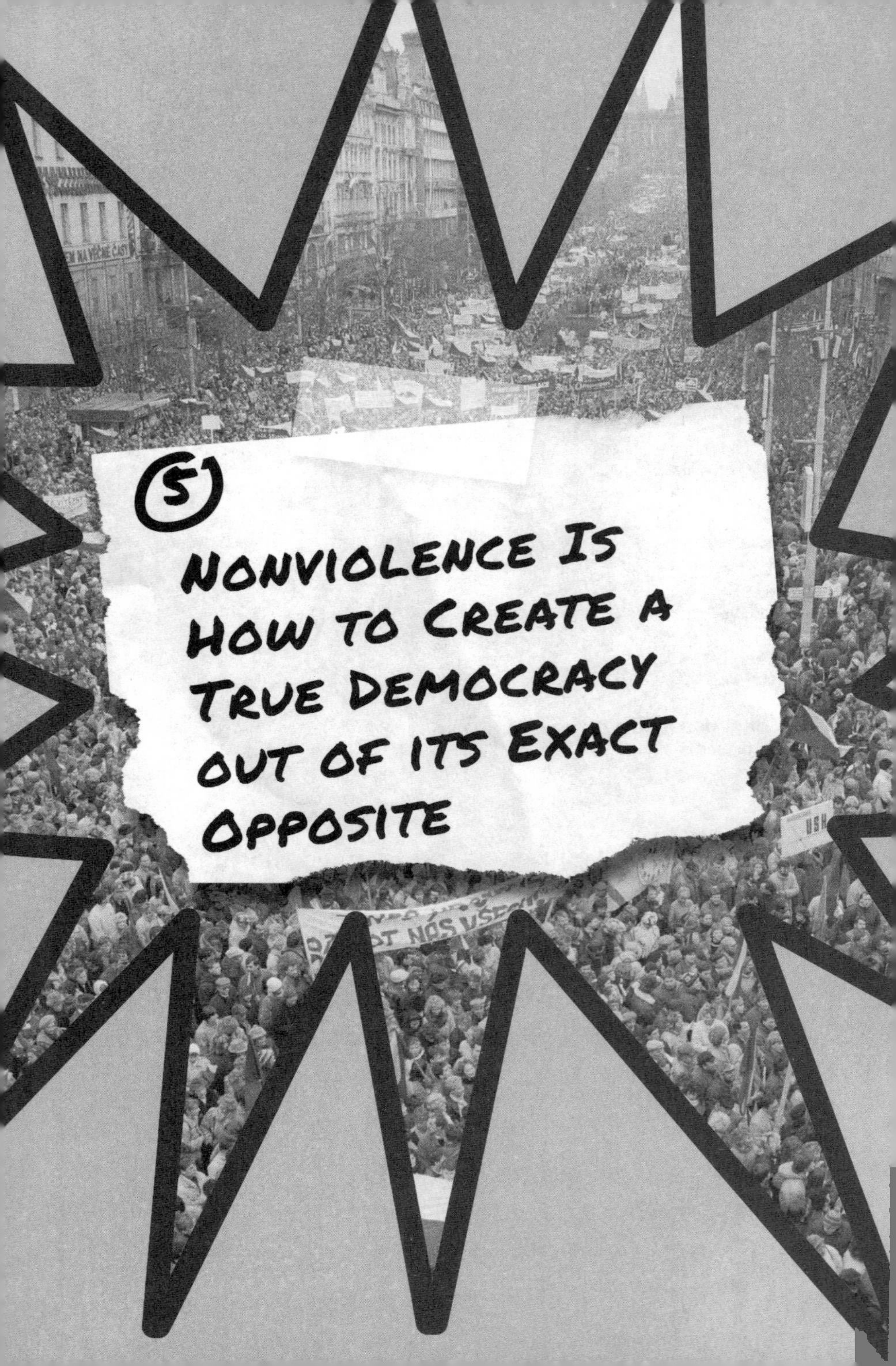

5 Nonviolence Is How to Create a True Democracy out of Its Exact Opposite

VÁCLAV HAVEL and the VELVET REVOLUTION

Václav Havel, playwright and dissident, addresses a crowd in 1988, less than a year before the Velvet Revolution would end over forty years of communist rule in Czechoslovakia.

"If the main pillar of the system is living a lie, then it is not surprising that the fundamental threat to it is living the truth."

—VÁCLAV HAVEL,
"THE POWER OF THE POWERLESS"

FRIDAY, NOVEMBER 17, 1989. A CLEAR, COOL DAY THAT THE setting sun would soon make cooler yet. At four in the afternoon, fifteen thousand students assembled in Prague, Czechoslovakia, for a demonstration. They received permission from the communist authorities, which was good, because without it such a gathering would be illegal.

In 1989 the people of Czechoslovakia lived under a totalitarian communist regime. And they had been since 1948. The government *totally* controlled everything and everyone.

Back in 1948, many Czechoslovakians welcomed communism. Still reeling from the nation's horrible experience of living under fascist Nazi occupation during World War II, these citizens believed, or at least hoped, that a communist society would bring them security and prosperity.

But in practice, this system created a much greater problem: life without freedom.

Simply put, the communist leadership claimed complete control of virtually every aspect of its citizens' lives. Freedom of expression and assembly were rights that did not exist in Czechoslovakia. Elections weren't democratic, and all media—newspapers, radio, television—were state-run and closely monitored. Censorship was rampant.

Worse yet, this lack of freedom didn't originate inside the country's borders. Choosing communism also meant siding with the Soviet Union (USSR) in its Cold War with the United States. Officially, Czechoslovakia and every other communist country across eastern and central Europe had its own government, but ultimately they had no choice but to obey orders coming from Moscow.

By 1989, many people in Czechoslovakia were sick and tired of communist rule. And so demonstrators came together on November 17 to push back, though they were not so bold as to advertise the gathering as an antigovernment protest.

Officially, this march was merely intended to mark fifty years since the death of Jan Opletal, a Czech student who was shot and killed during an anti-Nazi rally back in 1939. Opletal was a medical student, and the fifteen thousand students who met at the Institute of Pathology came to trace the path of his funeral procession. But it was clear that the marchers had much more in mind than just commemorating a decades-old death.

Dressed in the red, white, and blue of the Czechoslovakian tricolor flag, the students carried candles, carnations, and banners bearing bold messages: FREE ELECTIONS, DEMOCRACY AND LAW, and WHO IF NOT US? WHEN IF NOT NOW? In one speech, student Martin Klíma gave voice to the crowd's true priorities when he called out, "Today we shall not just piously remember; we are concerned about the present."

Saying you're concerned about the present might not sound risky, but in this country at this time it could lead to plenty of trouble: an interrogation with the secret police, an expulsion from school, even a visit to prison.

As the demonstrators made their way in the early evening to the National Cemetery, others joined them. Old, young, workers, parents, families, curious bystanders, citizens who hadn't dared challenge the government their entire lives. The steadily swelling procession was like a magnet, a force many couldn't resist. By the time the demonstrators reached Opletal's grave they numbered fifty thousand, making this the country's largest rally in twenty years.

The planned gathering, the one the government okayed, was supposed to end here, but the ever-growing crowd had other ideas. They continued marching along the River Vltava, winding through Prague, and heading toward Wenceslas Square, the epicenter of the country's public and political life. Wenceslas Square, a wide boulevard many blocks long, had played host to numerous pivotal demonstrations in the nation's history. Whoever controlled this stretch of real estate controlled the country. For decades now that had been the communist government, which held the occasional rally here, gatherings many attended only for fear of being noted as absent.

The first marchers passed the National Theatre and turned onto Národní Street, just blocks away from the square, only to be greeted by rows of helmeted riot police, who stood behind plexiglass shields with truncheons in their hands. After a few thousand civilians turned onto Národní, a second group of police cut them off from the rest of the demonstrators.

The protesters were surrounded.

A standoff began.

"We Don't Want Violence." Separated by an improvised "living altar," protestors and police confront each other on a night that would soon end in violence.

The students at the head of the procession held a banner that read WE DON'T WANT VIOLENCE. They sat down on the pavement and called out, "We have empty hands." They chanted the Czech version of the American civil rights movement anthem "We Shall Overcome." In the ten feet separating the unarmed civilians from the security forces, a living altar was built out of candles, illuminating the night. Students approached the police and offered them flowers.

An hour passed, and then another.

At 8:40 p.m., after repeatedly ordering everyone to disperse, the security forces set upon the demonstrators from both directions. Truncheons slammed into defenseless bodies. The fifteen hundred riot police, now supported by armored cars and police dogs, beat and kicked the trapped civilians. People were crushed into one another or suddenly found themselves pressed up against one of the buildings along Národní Street. Screams filled the air. Eventually the nonviolent demonstrators were allowed to escape through a single narrow alleyway, a fifty-foot-long escape route lined by club-wielding police on both sides.

The blood would be visible in the streets and on the walls of buildings for days to come.

Almost six hundred people were injured, their ages ranging from thirteen to eighty-three. Citizens who weren't there struggled to get reliable information about the confrontation, since the government controlled all news media. For a time, a rumor circulated that one person was killed. This turned out to be untrue, but it hardly mattered.

The public quickly named the evening of November 17 "the massacre."

•

The year 1989 wasn't the first time Czechoslovakians tried to address the problems with communism. In fact, in 1968, the government itself, led by Alexander Dubček, introduced reforms with the hope of transforming the country. Dubček believed that communism and democracy could coexist. His new program would create "socialism with a human face."

A Nonviolent Tradition. This general strike, part of a wave of passive resistance in 1968, didn't spare the country from Soviet repression, but it taught the people of Czechoslovakia valuable lessons they would call on twenty-one years later.

There would be greater freedom of expression. People would be allowed to gather in large numbers without government approval. Even the electoral laws would be changed.

The Prague Spring, as these series of reforms came to be known, was soon underway. Optimism swept the country.

But it wouldn't last long.

On August 20, 1968, more than a half-million troops from the USSR, Poland, East Germany, Hungary, and

Bulgaria, with orders to fire only if fired upon, invaded Czechoslovakia from every direction but the west with the aim of dismantling the Dubček government and reversing the reforms.

The 175,000-member Czechoslovakian army was formidable, but Dubček knew they had no chance against this massive invasion. Rather than participate in a bloody conflict, the Dubček government ordered the army to remain in its barracks and instructed the populace to meet the invaders with passive resistance, that is, nonviolence. Radio announcers told the people, "Whenever you meet members of the occupation forces do not allow open clashes to arise which might be regarded as provocations."

Civilians confronted soldiers in the streets, but with words not weapons, trying to persuade them to turn back. Human blockades stopped advancing tanks. In Prague, there were some violent confrontations, as tanks opened fire and demonstrators hurled Molotov cocktails. But those were the exceptions. Again and again Czechoslovakian citizens heeded the radio broadcasts: "Let your weapon be passive resistance. Don't be provoked into bloodshed. That's what they're waiting for. Don't be provoked."

Resistance, defiance, and noncooperation took

many forms. The statue at the center of Wenceslas Square was covered in Czechoslovakian flags and messages, in Russian, saying, "Soldiers, go home!" Mass demonstrations took place. General strikes were held. Railways were sabotaged to prevent the transportation of military equipment. Street signs were painted over or simply removed, until the only accurate sign in Prague read MOSCOW—1500 KILOMETERS.

The invading troops, confronted time and again by unarmed citizens pleading with them to leave their country, found their weapons nearly useless. Morale plummeted, until fresh troops had to be rotated in every four days.

By refusing to meet violence with violence, Czechoslovakia claimed the moral high ground in the conflict. The rest of the world saw clearly that this invasion went against the will of the Czechoslovakian people and its government, who had wanted nothing more than the freedom to shape the course that communism would take in their country.

By not participating in a conventional war but rather choosing nonviolent resistance, Czechoslovakia exposed the USSR as a country with no respect for the most fundamental value of the international political system: the independence of each and every nation.

The claim that all communists, whether in Prague or Moscow, were all equal members in a single struggle against the West was exposed as a lie.

Thanks to nonviolent resistance, fewer than one hundred people (in a country of 14 million) lost their lives. Stymied by a nation refusing to take up arms, the Soviets needed many months to attain what they assumed would take only days. Czechoslovakia also established a tradition of nonviolence it would build upon with awesome results two decades later.

None of which is to say that Czechoslovakia won this showdown. By April 1969, the Soviets had achieved their aims. Dubček, kidnapped at gunpoint and taken to Moscow for one-sided negotiations, was eventually removed from power and replaced by officials willing to obey Moscow without question.

The reform measures were undone.

The Prague Spring was dead.

Václav Havel never planned on becoming a politician. He was an artist and a thinker, a man who began writing wonderfully absurd plays in the 1960s that poked fun at the cost of conformity in a communist society. By the time of the Prague Spring, he was well known in Czechoslovakia and called for the creation of a "dignified counterpart of the Communist party." Like most everyone else, he was deeply disappointed by how things turned out. "The fun was definitely over," he would recall some years later.

The "fun" of the once-promising 1960s was replaced with "normalization," a "process of civilized violence." In order to assure that a second Prague Spring wouldn't happen, massive purges took place. Almost half a million members of the Czechoslovakian communist party were forced to resign their posts and positions. Anyone who seemed sympathetic with the reforms was out. The new government took similar aim at the media, the universities, theaters, and journals, installing their people at every turn.

At least one out of every ten people in Czechoslovakia was directly affected by the firings and demotions that swept the shocked and disillusioned country. Party officials became street sweepers. Children of reform advocates were kept out of the best schools. Former party members who continued to push for reform wound up in prison.

The message was clear: the government knows best and no dissent will be tolerated.

The new hardline communist regime now controlled everything from the military to the most minor literary journal. "Interrogations, house searches, phone tapping, the interception of private correspondence, unlawful detention, and eventually arrests, trials, and imprisonment" kept people in line, reminding them that even secret opposition would be exposed, and punished.

Unlike the vast majority of his fellow citizens, however, Havel refused to back down. Instead, he spoke out against the repressive regime. In an appearance on television in 1969, he spoke plainly. "There is just one road open to us: to wage our political battle until the end." Of course, Havel paid a steep price for statements like this. By 1971 he was prohibited from publishing new works, and his existing plays could no longer be produced inside his country's borders. In the years to come, he would be forced to perform manual labor, undergo constant police harassment, and endure multiple stays in prison.

Havel was not alone in his opposition, as there were eventually hundreds of other so-called dissidents, people who resisted government pressure in all sorts of ways. One such group aligned with the dissidents was precisely that, a group, of the rock 'n' roll variety. Formed less than a month after the 1968 invasion, they called themselves the Plastic People of the Universe.

Like everything else in Czechoslovakia, popular music was tightly regulated by the authorities. You could only sing certain kinds of songs with certain kinds of words. And you could only look a certain kind of way while you did this. If you wanted to perform, you would first have to play in front of a party functionary, who would then determine whether or not your act was worthy of a license permitting you to entertain your fellow citizens in public.

The Plastic People of the Universe would have none of that. Their rebellious music was about refusing to conform in every last way. They grew their hair long and dressed wildly, just like their musical role models in the West, who the communists especially despised. The Plastics played whatever they felt like playing, which was often loud, dark, and just plain weird.

Not surprisingly, this got them into trouble.

In March 1976, the secret police broke up one of their concerts, arresting the Plastics, along with their manager, a poet and art historian named Ivan Jirous, plus a number of others. The trial of Jirous and three band members (the rest were released) took place in September, and when it was over they were found guilty of disturbing the peace or "aggravated hooliganism." Jirous was sentenced to eighteen months in prison. The others received sentences between eight months and a year. Upon their release, the band would get back together and continue making music, and occasionally getting in trouble with the authorities, for years to come.

Václav Havel didn't like the Plastics' actual music all that much, but he was outraged by the regime's willingness to punish the performers for nothing more than artistic self-expression. "They were simply young people," Havel wrote, "who wanted to live in their own way, to make music they liked, to sing what they wanted to sing, to live in harmony with themselves, and to express themselves in a truthful way."

Havel and a number of other dissidents—artists, scholars, journalists, and former members of Dubček's government—gathered to figure out how to respond to living under a regime that would treat the Plastics as they had. The only thing uniting this diverse group was their conviction that they could no longer remain silent. The result was a document named Charter 77, which called on the government to honor the international human rights agreements it had signed over the years. These agreements, such as the International Covenant on Civil and Politics Rights, which the government signed in 1966, committed the communist leadership to respecting a wide-range of basic individual rights, including freedom of speech and the right to a fair trial.

By early January 1977, 243 people had signed the charter. On the sixth of that month, Havel and two other men, actor Pavel Landovský and writer Ludvík Vaculík, went to deliver a copy to the Federal Assembly and mail copies to all the signers. But the secret police had learned of their plan, possibly by bugging another dissident's apartment. The seemingly simple task of distributing these copies would turn out to be anything but.

Just before noon, the three men climbed inside an old Saab. Landovský was behind the wheel, while Havel rode shotgun and Vaculík sat in back. Not long after setting off down the snowy streets, they were already being followed by four cars driven by the secret police. Landovský "hit the gas," taking the car up to seventy miles an hour as it sped through downtown Prague. Additional police cars joined the chase at nearly every intersection.

When Landovský suddenly swerved onto a side street, one that hadn't been salted, two police cars lost control and crashed into each other. This gave the Saab just enough time to screech to a halt in front of a nearby mailbox. Havel hopped out of the car and stuffed around forty envelopes into it before racing back to the car and hopping inside. The car sped away, the police already in pursuit once again. Only a few blocks later two police cars appeared in front of the Saab, cutting off its route. Soon they were surrounded. The three men were taken into custody, and the remaining copies of the declaration were confiscated. But it hardly mattered, for the Charter had already been leaked to sympathizers and journalists in countries throughout the West.

Because the Internet didn't exist yet, Charter 77 wasn't suddenly available everywhere all at once, but nevertheless, the declaration soon began appearing in publications abroad, where it received considerable attention. The charter clearly stated that its signers did not view themselves as a political opposition, but were merely civilians who wanted to have an honest dialogue about human and civil rights with the state authorities. As the charter put it, their aim, above all, was "to help enable all the citizens of Czechoslovakia to work and live as free human beings."

Despite this understandable objective, the Charter 77 members were treated like enemies of the state. Many of them, including Havel, were brought in for repeated interrogations that would last all day, day after day, for a month or more. One member of Charter 77, the sixty-nine-year-old Jan Patočka, considered one of the great philosophers of the twentieth century, eventually suffered a fatal heart attack under the stress of these interrogations.

The communist regime simply would not tolerate dissent. Even peaceful dialogue was out of the question.

If this was the truth of the situation, what could one possibly do? How could a powerless citizen resist such a powerful totalitarian regime?

The answer: live this truth.

After the Charter 77 showdown, Havel recognized that influencing politics directly was out of the question. The government's power in this realm was absolute. Nevertheless, Havel continued resisting the tyrannical communists and often turned to the written word not just to voice his opposition, but to teach his fellow citizens how they could and why they must resist as well. Despite the current dire situation, Havel felt there was much to be done, because, he believed, even a totalitarian regime is vulnerable.

In his most famous essay, "The Power of the Powerless," Havel tells the story of a greengrocer who hangs the well-known communist slogan "Workers of the world, unite!" in the window of his store. He doesn't do this because he believes in the slogan. Like everyone else, he knows that there's no connection between communism's lofty ideals and the ruthlessness of its government. But the greengrocer pretends he believes, because pretending makes his life easier.

By publicly showing the authorities, the secret police, and the anonymous informers they rely on (informers who could very well be his next-door neighbors) that he obeys, the greengrocer spares himself a lot of trouble. He lies to prove his obedience, because lying is a small price to pay to avoid harassment, or worse.

But, Havel argues, the lie of putting up this slogan has additional effects. The greengrocer's lie causes others to lie as well. He pretends, and by pretending he forces other shopkeepers to pretend. Together they all must live the lie, giving the empty ideology behind the lie—communism—enormous strength.

As it turns out, all these reluctant liars aren't just victims of this system, they *are* the system, or at least a crucial part of it. The government needs everyone's cooperation to enjoy complete power. Without this kind of massive, countrywide peer pressure, the entire system would fall apart.

But there is an alternative.

The greengrocer can choose to behave otherwise; he can "live within the truth." He can refuse to put up the sign. He can share his honest opinion at a public meeting. He can say he supports those who have spoken out before him.

Make no mistake, if he does these things, the greengrocer will be punished. He will lose his job or get demoted. His children might not be able to attend college. The luxuries made available to obedient citizens, a summer vacation for instance, will no longer be his to enjoy. But, according to Havel, these sacrifices will be worth it, since this is how one can effectively resist.

The entire system "works only as long as people are willing to live within the lie."

Like so many great nonviolent leaders before and after him, Havel understood how power truly operates. Power isn't, as we often believe, something only the powerful possess, a tool they use to control those below them, the powerless. No, power is actually a particular kind of *relationship*. The powerful demand obedience and the powerless comply: they do what is expected of them. But if the so-called powerless refuse to obey, the powerful are no different from anyone else.

Hence the title of Havel's essay: "The Power of the Powerless."

Of course, things aren't quite that simple. The powerful often have tools of other sorts, like laws, policemen, and prisons, tools that strongly encourage the powerless to do what they're told, tools the powerful can use to make the powerless suffer if they challenge their role in the relationship. Despite this, it's always possible to choose not to obey, and to choose to suffer the consequences instead.

The things one had to obey and the consequences one would suffer for refusing to obey in Czechoslovakia were nearly endless in the late 1970s. But this was in fact the weakness of the country's totalitarian system: It sought complete control of everything. *Everything*. Not just how people acted politically, but what they said and even thought in areas that seemed to have nothing to do with politics at all. The music they listened to, the books they read, the subjects they discussed with their friends.

So, Havel argued, resistance needed to begin in those places, where people could choose to live the truth. People had to use the power they did have to carve out little areas of freedom for themselves, in their minds, in their interactions with people in their communities, in the small acts of everyday life.

Havel believed the truth could be very dangerous. Why? Because, as he put it, "if the main pillar of the system is living a lie, then it is not surprising that the fundamental threat to it is living the truth."

The true battleground for power in Czechoslovakia would start not within the government, the military, or even the newspapers, Havel wrote in 1978. No, the first battle would take place in the mind and private world of each individual.

Each individual who chooses to live in the truth will come to act on this in some way or another. By signing a letter demanding intellectual freedom, by attending the concert of an underground rock group, by speaking their mind honestly at a political gathering, which up to this point had merely been another exercise in living the lie.

Together all these acts will add up to a "nonviolent attempt by people to negate the system within themselves." Living in the truth will begin with each individual realizing that he or she does in fact have power in the small decisions of everyday life, and thus, the responsibility to choose truth over lies.

Havel's notion of living in the truth sounds a lot like Gandhi's satyagraha or truth force. Like Gandhi before him, Havel saw that above all "the prime human obligation is to act fearlessly and publicly in accord with one's beliefs."

This is why, for Havel, living in the truth meant resisting oppression nonviolently whenever possible.

One had to stop cooperating with the regime, because cooperation was wrong. But to replace violence with violence would be to accept a different kind of lie: that the way one acquires power has no effect on how one uses it. "A future secured by violence," he wrote, "might actually be worse than what exists now."

Havel knew that the regime would try to cover up the power of the truth with more lies, and for a long time it would appear that the truth was losing. But over time the truth would rot the system of lies from the inside out, until the truth finally burst forth victorious. In the end, Havel predicted back in 1978, this victory, whenever it comes, would occur suddenly and unexpectedly.

This prediction would turn out to be absolutely, astoundingly true, with even Havel himself being surprised when victory finally arrived. More than a decade later, in September 1989, he said that he hoped change was coming, but that "we might not live to see the day." The massacre occurred just two months later, and at first it seemed like just one more defeat for truth and freedom.

But the truth of the matter would be just the opposite. Because the rotting was almost complete.

•

Saturday morning, November 18, 1989. Only twelve hours had passed since the massacre. Stunned and confused students throughout Prague were frantically trying to determine their next steps. Thanks to the government's control of the news, many still didn't know what precisely had happened the night before. But the theater department students at the Academy of Performing Arts in Prague were already taking a stand. They wrote a proclamation calling for a weeklong strike and demanding a government inquiry into the massacre. By early afternoon the proclamation was read aloud in Prague's Realistické Theater, where four hundred directors, playwrights, theater managers, and actors from across the capital had gathered.

Curtains would soon rise on Saturday matinees throughout the city. The theater had long filled a central role in Czechoslovakian culture, and many workers and their families would be attending plays this day. But the theater professionals decided to align themselves with the students and support their demands by declaring a weeklong strike of their own. The new alliance chose November 27 as the date for a nationwide general strike.

When audiences arrived at theaters throughout the city, instead of a performance, they heard the students' proclamation announcing the strike. In theater after theater, the crowds responded with enthusiastic applause. In some venues, everyone sang the national anthem, which gave way to moments of silence. By the end of the day, theaters across the country had joined the strike.

In the fight over control of Prague's public spaces, which began at Wenceslas Square the night before, the people had claimed new turf: the city's theaters. There would be no performances for the foreseeable future. Instead, these large halls would host regular discussions, meetings, and educational sessions, as people rediscovered the courage to speak openly about the kind of society they wanted in their country. The country's theaters transformed into the headquarters for the nation's return to democracy.

And just as all this was set in motion, Václav Havel, who had left Prague before Friday's demonstration in order to avoid being detained by the authorities yet again, returned to the capital.

By Monday, November 20, he was the head of a new organization, the Civic Forum (CF), a loose alliance of academics, artists, one-time reformists, and even a few industrial workers. Most of CF's leaders, including Havel himself, were dissidents, people who had openly opposed the communists for years, and at great personal cost. CF would soon represent the people in their effort to negotiate with the communist leadership, and their first step in this process was adopting a declaration, written by Havel, that demanded the following:

- The resignation of communist officials involved in the 1968 invasion
- The resignation of officials responsible for the violence on November 17
- An independent investigation into the events of November 17
- The immediate release of all prisoners of conscience held for speaking out against the government

And this wasn't the only major development that Monday. On the same cold, overcast day, 150,000 demonstrators, most of them students, finally captured Wenceslas Square. One survivor of the massacre explained their collective boldness by saying, "We were now more angry than afraid." They jangled their keys, as if to ring a bell, signaling that time was up for the communist leadership. They chanted as well. "Freedom!" "Resign!" "This is it!" and "We have had enough!"

This time the police did nothing.

Art galleries and cinemas followed the theaters' lead, shutting down their exhibitions and turning off their projectors. Instead their spaces hosted spontaneous gatherings, where newly energized citizens shared information, floated ideas, formed committees, and planned for the future.

Here and elsewhere, artists, along with amateur activists, drew up posters, handbills, and banners by the thousands that were soon plastered over public spaces far and wide. University buildings, shop windows, Metro stations, the walls of the National Museum, even the statue of St. Wenceslas himself became sites for exchanging and spreading ideas, something that remained vital, since the government still controlled TV, radio, and newspapers.

"AN END TO ONE PARTY RULE."

"WE WANT DEMOCRACY."

"THE HEART OF EUROPE CRIES FOR FREEDOM."

"TRUTH WILL PREVAIL."

"UNITY IS STRENGTH."

Ideas that for so long couldn't be shared out in the open now covered much of the country. Czechoslovakia was quickly being wallpapered in free expression.

On Tuesday, November 21, a day that started with snow but turned sunny by afternoon, the crowd in Wenceslas Square was bigger yet: two hundred thousand. Many more regular civilians, including some workers, now stood and chanted alongside the students.

The time came to address the crowd, but from where? A balcony in a building belonging to the Socialist Party of Czechoslovakia that looked out onto the square was a perfect spot. True, the organization was a front for the Communist Party, but thankfully its leader, Jan Skoda, was a friend of Havel's from his school days and a member of the Civic Forum, so he offered them access.

Of course, with a crowd this size, simply shouting down from above wasn't going to do the trick. This was when one of the more unlikely advantages of having a revolution led by artists and performers revealed itself. In no time "stagehands, sound technicians, and stage managers of various rock 'n' roll bands" appeared with the necessary equipment and set up speakers that one member of the gigantic crowd described as "amazingly loud and clear."

A diverse mix of speakers addressed the jubilant

masses, the crowd seeing itself in the faces on the balcony. Students, workers, actors, and dissidents, such as the Catholic priest Václav Malý, who had been punished again and again for speaking out against the regime, made their voices heard. And the sound system didn't amplify only words. Musicians also played from the balcony, including a number of legendary performers who hadn't been seen in public since the days of the Prague Spring.

In 1968, Marta Kubišová was one of the most popular singers in the country. But she was banned from performing for refusing to cooperate with the authorities in 1970, not long after invoking both Gandhi and Martin Luther King Jr. in a music video. Suddenly, almost twenty years later, she stepped out onto the balcony. She was no longer so young, but it was definitely her. The crowd, some with tears in their eyes, others with their hands raised to make the victory sign, listened to her sing their national anthem unaccompanied. Just her powerful voice, reclaiming the national lyric as it floated out over the perfectly silent crowd.

Since returning to Prague early on Saturday, Havel had been busy around the clock helping to found and lead the Civic Forum. The headquarters of the CF was, fittingly, the Magic Lantern theater, barely a ten-minute walk from Wenceslas Square, at least on days when a sea of people wasn't flooding all the streets in between. Down a few flights of stairs and through a couple easy-to-miss, currently well-guarded doors at the Magic Lantern lay the revolution's headquarters, previously known as dressing rooms numbers ten and eleven.

Havel had waited decades for the cracks in the edifice of the totalitarian regime to appear. Well, here they were, deeper than anyone expected and yawning wider by the minute. If the masses continued shaking its fractured pillars, the enormous, long-intimidating communist tower would topple altogether.

On Tuesday, November 23, Havel walked up the many flights of stairs leading out of the underground Magic Lantern and up to street level. He made his way to the balcony overlooking the square and addressed the masses. People were already chanting, "Havel to the Castle!"—the Prague Castle in this case, their version of the White House—but he spoke humbly to his people. Refusing to simply grab the power now available to him, Havel instead emphasized the democratic spirit of the Civic Forum:

> I am a writer, not any sort of expert speaker. I will speak only briefly. Civic Forum is thought of as a spontaneous and temporary representation of the critical, thoughtful public. Anyone may spontaneously join who feels that they are a member.

There was joy and excitement down below, but impatience and anger, too. Indeed, one slogan the crowd chanted over and over again was "We have had enough."

The powerless would soon be the powerful. How would they respond? Would they demand revenge? Would they seek to inflict some of the suffering they had all endured on the people who had doled it out to them?

Havel, who for years had expressed the moral need to speak the truth, now reminded his people, in his gruff voice, that their revolution had to remain nonviolent. His voice called out through the speakers, referring to the regime and all its many collaborators. "Those who have for many years engaged in a violent and bloody vengefulness against their opponents are now afraid of us. They should rest easy. We are not like them."

These last words—we are not like them—weren't made up by Havel on the spot. No, this was another slogan heard again and again down in the square and seen papered all across the country. Havel emphasized this message, and in the process revealed a unique feature of this uprising, one responsible for its nonviolent nature.

The crowd wanted to replace one government with another, and in this way the daily demonstrations in Wenceslas Square were *political* events. But the Velvet Revolution—as these November events would come to be known by 1990, the term coined by translator and dissident Rita Klímová—was much more than this. These demonstrations, along with all the other public gatherings spreading across Czechoslovakia, were part of a *moral* revolution, a revolution about what people should value and how these values should influence their behavior. Perhaps the most central idea of the entire revolution—the only one that could be said to matter even more than nonviolence—was something called, in Czech, l'udskost', or "humanness."

The Velvet Revolution delivered humanness to Czechoslovakia, where it had been absent for at least twenty years.

Under the communist regime, living in Czechoslovakia was inhuman.

The lying was inhuman, putting people in jail for

playing rock music was inhuman, the violence was inhuman, the totalitarian government itself was inhuman.

The crowd's rejection of their communist government was a rejection not just of its power, but of the immoral way it used power. The government's power was dishonest, cruel, intimidating, and full of hatred, even for those who respectfully disagreed with it. The Velvet Revolution rejected all of this.

We are not like them.

The nonviolent Velvet Revolution would be successful because when the masses refuse to obey their leaders, these leaders are powerless. But the millions of ordinary citizens who participated in the Velvet Revolution *chose* nonviolence in the first place because it allowed them to show the difference between themselves and the government that oppressed them for decades.

Make no mistake, there were some who were already committed to nonviolence before the massacre. Havel, many of his dissident allies, and those students who wrote "We don't want violence" on their banners before the demonstration began on November 17. They were just a small minority, but their suffering in the massacre converted their fellow citizens to nonviolence, suddenly and absolutely.

The government's violent actions had backfired, uniting an entire nation behind a conviction to fight without taking up arms. Whatever the authorities stood for, whatever they did, the people would choose the opposite.

Hence another popular slogan: "Truth and love must win over lies and hate," itself reflected in a statement made by the CF: "Let us refuse any form of terror and violence. Our weapons are love and nonviolence."

The Velvet Revolution may well have been the most idealistic revolution of the twentieth century. Which would explain not only why it was led by students and artists—two groups often accused of not living in the "real world"—but why the country as a whole would soon elect a playwright with no experience in government to be its president.

But wait—why didn't the communist government do anything? What about all those tools the powerful have to force obedience? Just a few days earlier they had shown their power by calling upon a massive police force that brutally attacked the demonstrators. Yet after the massacre on November 17 there wouldn't be a single additional incident of violent government repression, not even so much as a lone policeman clubbing a defenseless demonstrator.

Nothing.

The government still controlled a potent cluster of security forces: the police, the secret police, various civilian militias, and, of course, the army itself. With the exception of a small minority of public dissidents, these forces had effectively kept the entire population in line for years.

So why didn't the government utilize them again? Why did they simply give up?

There had been crucial developments beyond the borders of Czechoslovakia that not only uplifted the opposition but deflated the government as well. A few years earlier, Mikhail Gorbachev became the leader of the Soviet Union and introduced monumental reforms to his country. Even more relevant, earlier in 1989 he announced that his country would no longer interfere with the paths chosen by other communist states. In other words, there wouldn't be another Soviet-led invasion like the one that rocked Czechoslovakia back in 1968.

Indeed, radical changes were afoot throughout central Europe. Poland, East Germany, and Hungary had all recently thrown off their Soviet shackles. The Berlin

Wall, which separated communist East Berlin from free West Berlin and stood as a symbol of communist oppression for almost thirty years, was torn down on November 9, 1989.

If living the truth was hollowing out the regime from the inside, then the changes in the international arena were applying incredible pressure from the outside.

Sooner or later the government in Czechoslovakia, perhaps the most repressive of all the European communist regimes, was going to be replaced. But there was no guarantee that it would happen quickly or nonviolently, yet the Velvet Revolution lasted less than a month and claimed not a single life.

So why did the government give up without a fight in just a matter of days?

The answer was not that they never considered using force. Something called Operation Intervention, involving thousands of soldiers and dozens of tanks, was planned at the army's highest level. But it was never implemented, even though it would have been simple enough to shed more civilian blood and possibly drive the uprising back underground again.

To understand why the government chose to surrender rather than fight a battle against an unarmed opponent they most certainly would defeat, here are some related incidents, all of which took place within a week of the massacre:

- Security forces ordered students to remove posters from the walls of university buildings. When the students didn't follow their commands, the police let it go.
- The governing committees of both the plainclothes state security forces and the Prague police submitted signed statements calling on the government to find a "political solution to the problem that has arisen in state and society."
- In these same statements, the security forces said they wouldn't intervene in future demonstrations unless party officials at the highest level accepted responsibility for the outcomes beforehand.
- The People's Militia, a well-armed force of at least fifty thousand workers organized by the communist party, was called upon to "deal with the antisocialist circles," that is, crack down on the demonstrators. It refused.

What do these incidents teach us? It's tempting to think of all the security forces that did the government's dirty work as little more than parts of an efficient, reliable machine that could be set in motion with the push of a button. But these forces were made up of real people, and every time they acted—by spying on a neighbor, sealing off a street, spraying a crowd with tear gas, or beating a protester—they first had to choose to obey the commands of their superiors.

This would explain why, during the first few days of the Velvet Revolution, the soldiers who would have been mobilized to carry out Operation Intervention were confined to their barracks, allowed no visitors, and kept away from all media. If they got word of what was happening, they might have decided to switch sides. Because all those soldiers in their identical uniforms were actually individual people, not robots.

These incidents tell us one more crucial and often overlooked aspect about the very nature of power.

Officers, generals, and politicians' "tools"—their soldiers and policemen—only provide their superiors with power when those in uniform follow orders. The moment they disobey, the instant they no longer agree to cooperate, these tools are useless and the once mighty are powerless.

This is precisely what happened in Czechoslovakia.

When Ladislav Adamec, the prime minister, agreed to negotiate with CF, when he announced that force

The Prime Minister and the Playwright. After punishing the dissident writer for years, Prime Minister Adamec (left) finally agrees to meet with Václav Havel (right), leader of the popular uprising, on November 26.

would not be used to restore order, all of which he did less than a week after the massacre, he was acknowledging that his power ultimately came from the people, and that he relied on some of these people (the police and the army) to keep the rest of the people (the civilian population) in line.

The civilians stopped obeying the rules and the police were threatening to defect to their side. Just like that, the government was powerless. And Adamec knew it.

There's another related reason the communist authorities avoided violence in the days following the massacre. Now that brute force wasn't an option, they realized their only hope was compromise. Perhaps, despite all their previous acts of violence, they could still share power.

Havel's nonviolent language suggested this may be possible. CF called for dialogue and democracy, not a total destruction of the current regime. When Havel said publicly, "There must not be a hunt for Communists. There must be justice but not revenge," he was giving the communists hope that they might be able to work together after all.

Bringing in the tanks would ruin all that, so they didn't.

Instead, at the invitation of Havel and the CF, Prime Minister Adamec addressed the masses on Sunday, November 26, the day he finally agreed to meet with Havel for the first time. The crowd was now so large—750 thousand—that Wenceslas Square had been left behind for the sprawling Letna Park on the other side of the river. Havel called for a "dialogue of power with

SOVĚTSKÝM SVAZEM NA VĚČNÉ ČASY
PODPORUJEME OBČANSKÉ FÓRUM
MEX
USH
ORWO

the public," suggesting that the current communist government might remain in some form, but when Adamec spoke he sought to dictate the terms of the coming general strike, as if he were still the one calling the shots.

Among the crowd, "applause turned to" disapproving "whistles." Long used to wielding absolute power, Adamec had no idea how to share it. Just like that, the opportunity for this corrupt government to save itself had come and gone. The people finally understood the power they had, and they weren't about to share with those who had abused it so horribly for years.

Monday, November 27. Ten days had passed since the massacre, and today a new Czechoslovakia, busy reinventing itself, would act as one.

At exactly noon, sirens and bells sounded across the country. Half of the working population of the country went on strike, while another fourth (such as hospital employees who couldn't stop working) observed the event in symbolic fashion.

People went on strike in a variety of ways. Many gathered in their town squares. Some took down

People Power. On November 27, half of all workers went on strike to support the revolution.

empty communist slogans from the walls of their workplaces or the roofs of their factories. Teachers discussed politics with their students, openly. Many sang the national anthem.

And in some cases, paradoxically, people went on strike by working, only better or harder than they normally worked. As Milan Kňažko, an actor and leading figure in the revolution, said on television just a few days before the strike: "Bakers, your strike is the tricolor, and bread more fragrant than other times . . . Journalists and filmmakers, let your general strike be to speak the truth." In a sense, the strike was the first time the population of revolutionary Czechoslovakia could fully be this new, better version of itself. Dignified, kind, friendly, generous, honest, and nonviolent. Indeed, many of those who went on strike for two hours ultimately gave back those two hours to their employees, but without asking for additional pay in return.

Two days later, on November 29, the Federal Assembly struck from the constitution the clause guaranteeing the Communist Party a leading role in society. Negotiations between the communists and the CF continued, until on December 3, the government announced that it would form a new cabinet. This sounded like good news, but the announcement said that the cabinet would have fifteen communist and five noncommunist members. Adamec and his people, long used to being in control, were blind to the writing on the walls.

The CF called for another general strike in response.

But this wasn't necessary, as Adamec, finally coming to his senses, resigned altogether on December 6. Four days later, on December 10, President Husak swore in a new Government of National Understanding and then promptly resigned. It was the first noncommunist government in Czechoslovakia in forty-one years.

Only twenty-four days had passed since the massacre on November 17.

Near the end of the month, on December 29, the new Parliament met and elected Václav Havel as president. He would be reelected to the position in a democratic, national election in June of the following year.

On January 1, 1990, President Václav Havel addressed the nation. The New Year's speech was a tradition in Czechoslovakia, and despite the revolution that just ended, some things would stay the same. Havel now resided in the magnificent Prague Castle, the largest ancient castle in all of Europe, and the past home of not just communist tyrants but actual kings as well. In the months to come, this most unusual leader would host unusual visitors, like the Rolling Stones, but today he had to be presidential.

"My dear fellow citizens," he began:

> For forty years you heard from my predecessors on this day different variations on the same theme: how our country was flourishing, how many million tons of steel we produced, how happy we all were, how we trusted our government, and what bright perspectives were unfolding in front of us. I assume you did not propose me for this office so that I, too, would lie to you. Our country is not flourishing.

The Velvet Revolution was a time of euphoria for an entire country, as an oppressed people toppled a despised regime in less than a month without taking up arms. But the time for celebrating had reached its end, as vast amounts of challenging work now awaited the nation. After forty years of dishonest leadership that wouldn't acknowledge the country's problems, let alone tackle them, Czechoslovakia's economy and infrastructure had been left in a "catastrophic state." It might have been nice to pretend otherwise, to let

Havel to the Castle. On December 10, Václav Havel waves to a crowd of people in Wenceslas Square, the epicenter of the Velvet Revolution.

the celebration last a while longer, but Havel, ever devoted to the truth, once more decided to tell it like it is.

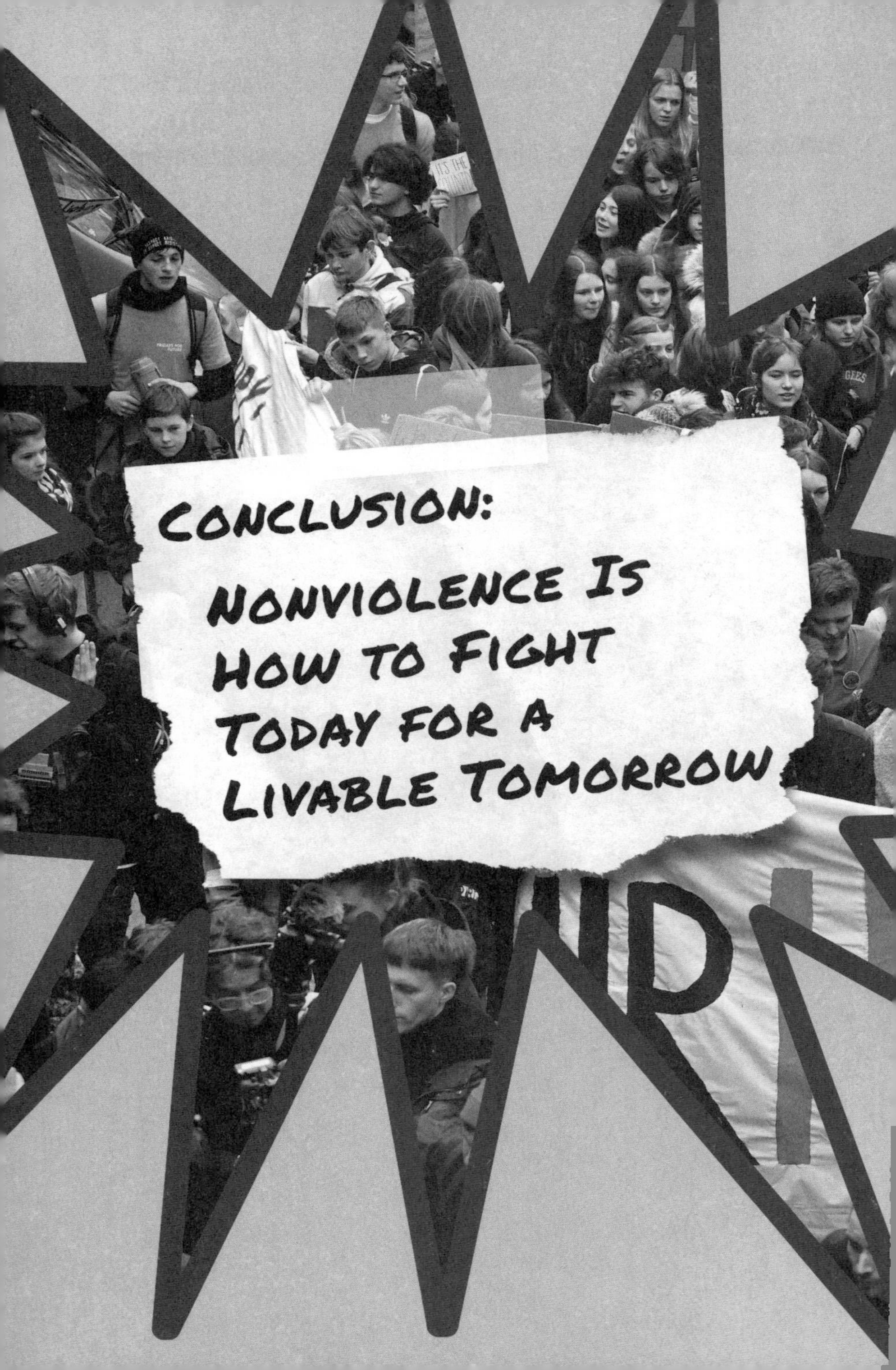

Conclusion:

Nonviolence Is How to Fight Today for a Livable Tomorrow

GRETA THUNBERG and the CLIMATE CHANGE MOVEMENT

Fifteen-year-old Swedish student Greta Thunberg, near the beginning of her school strike to raise awareness about climate change, in August 2018

"Hope is not something that you have. Hope is something that you create, with your actions. Hope is something you have to manifest into the world, and once one person has hope, it can be contagious."

—CONGRESSWOMAN ALEXANDRIA OCASIO-CORTEZ IN CONVERSATION WITH GRETA THUNBERG

ON DECEMBER 5, 2018, A GIRL ROSE BEHIND A PODIUM IN Katowice, Poland, her hair braided into two long pigtails resting on her chest. After adjusting the microphone's height, she spoke: "My name is Greta Thunberg. I am fifteen years old, and I'm from Sweden." Her voice was not particularly loud and at first it was easy to wonder what in the world this young person, rather small for her age, was doing at the United Nations Climate Change Conference, delivering a speech to leaders from around the world.

Thunberg would soon justify her presence. Like so

many great nonviolent leaders before her, from Gandhi to Havel, she had come to share a potent truth:

> Solving the climate crisis is the greatest and most complex challenge that homo sapiens have ever faced. The main solution, however, is so simple that even a small child can understand it. We have to stop the emissions of greenhouse gases.

Throughout this book, we have seen two central principles of nonviolent resistance guide movements from India to Alabama and from California to Czechoslovakia:

1. Speak your truth, whether or not others want to hear it.
2. Act on your beliefs, even if this requires sacrifice and the disruption of a system those in power intend to preserve.

The second of these should be obvious by now. Over the course of the twentieth century, nonviolent activists refused to back down when their calls for change were ignored. Instead, they confronted unjust authorities and willingly suffered as a result. Activists endured long marches, hours upon hours of protest, and hunger strikes. They faced vicious dogs, brutal beatings, trips to prison, and even attempts on their lives. All this in the name of furthering their cause.

But what does the truth have to do with this? Why exactly does the truth matter so much to these movements?

And it matters, to be sure. Near the very beginning of the decades he would devote to nonviolent activism, Gandhi articulated the deep connection between truth and nonviolence. The name he gave to both his philosophy and political strategy, satyagraha, made this absolutely clear. "Satya" means truth, while "agraha" means holding firmly. When it came to nonviolence, Gandhi emphasized the truth, not peacefulness, above all else.

Still, it's easy, in a book about *past* nonviolent movements, movements that have already changed the world, to underappreciate truth's fundamental role in such activism. After all, in the twenty-first century, it's common to claim that no nation should colonize another, that women deserve the vote just like men, that the color of one's skin shouldn't determine one's rights, and on and on. Indeed, today these beliefs may well be held by a sizable majority of people around the world.

Yet these and other truths were once radical. In 1910, the colonization of India was widely accepted. In 1950, many saw segregation as the proper order of American society, just as they had seen the disenfranchisement of women as perfectly reasonable a half century earlier. Many people, people who benefited from what Václav Havel called "living the lie," did everything in their power to prevent others from seeing these truths for what they were.

Put differently, the civil rights movement's accomplishments include not just the end of legal government-supported segregation. This movement also turned a certain truth, once controversial and often dismissed, into a mainstream view. Today only extremists challenge the notion, so aptly expressed by Martin Luther King Jr., that each and every person should be judged not by the color of their skin but by the content of their character.

Which isn't to say that such extremists are now powerless, or that their views will necessarily be considered extreme forever. In fact, the last few years have seen a troubling rise in racism at the highest level of both American and European politics, while democracy is actually weaker throughout much of eastern Europe in 2019 than it was at the end of 1989. Some truths, even after appearing to emerge victorious, may need to be fought for all over again.

Related to this, the victory for a truth in one place doesn't mean it will automatically prevail elsewhere. Freedom of expression, for instance, remains mostly out of reach in places like China, North Korea, and Russia. And though we might assume that the victory of one truth should lead to people embracing other related truths, this, unfortunately, isn't always the case. In the United States, to take just one example, women have the vote, but remain less equal than men when it comes to pay and still only represent one in five members of Congress.

The world is a much better place thanks to the nonviolent movements of the last hundred years, but it's far from perfect and we shouldn't assume that the gains these activists have won can never be lost. The truth won't fight for itself just because others are championing a lie.

What is certain, however, is that when we turn our attention to a current, ongoing nonviolent movement, we find activists struggling not just to influence politicians, but first and foremost to get these leaders, along with regular people everywhere, to acknowledge the truth that makes this movement necessary to begin with. Often this truth won't even be controversial yet, it will be marginal, the kind of thing most people easily ignore and dismiss altogether. And this is exactly the case when it comes to the effort to stop global warming.

Greta Thunberg is a satyagrahi, one who holds firmly to her truth: Climate change is real, so real it threatens our collective future. She believes that once enough people confront and accept the full force of this alarming truth that action will follow. So she speaks this truth wherever and whenever she can, and she disrupts the routine in order to increase and draw attention to her opportunities to do precisely that.

Greta Thunberg didn't become a global spokesperson for climate activism overnight, though her rise to prominence has been stunningly swift, a case of the exact right person emerging at the exact right time. Still, she started as most activists do, by confronting a distressing, unpopular truth and choosing to act on it locally.

When Greta first learned about climate change, at the age of eight, she wondered how people could care about anything other than this massive, pressing problem. If the warnings are accurate—and the scientific findings are not only overwhelming; the reality of climate change already appears to be upon us—if hundreds of millions, perhaps even billions, of lives will be jeopardized by higher temperatures, rising seas, and widespread drought; if entire cities might become uninhabitable; if time is running out for us to reduce the carbon emissions causing global warming, then why, she wondered, aren't people around the world doing everything in their power to reduce these emissions?

But Greta was unlike almost everyone else, young or old, in her refusal to move past this initial shock,

Speak Your Truth. "School Strike for Climate": Fifteen-year-old Swedish student Greta Thunberg near the beginning of her school strike to raise awareness about climate change, in August 2018.

return to her daily routine, and pretend there was nothing she could do. No, Greta was different. She was unable to think of anything else. She fell into a deep depression and stopped eating. She read everything she could on the topic, driven by a need to understand this painful truth completely. Slowly she began to speak out. First at home, in her eventually successful efforts to convince her parents to become vegans and stop traveling by plane.

As she entered her teens, however, it was no longer enough for her to influence her parents only. She needed to bring her message to the public. After all, Greta believed that the time had come to act like one does in the middle of an emergency. She felt, as she would put it in another speech, that "our house is on fire." And she was barely exaggerating, since the worst forest fires in Sweden's modern history, fires caused by a combination of record-high temperatures and drought, ravaged the country throughout the summer of 2018.

Greta became inspired by young gun-control activists in the United States who had started another recent nonviolent movement—March for Our Lives. These activists "refused to go to school because of the . . . shootings"; so, too, Greta stopped attending school on

Fridays in the fall of 2018. Instead, she went on a climate strike in front of the Swedish Parliament in Stockholm.

On the first day it was just Greta and a sign that read SCHOOL STRIKE FOR THE CLIMATE. But on the second day she was joined by another protester. As Greta put it, "The step from one to two is the hardest step, and once you've taken that step you're not far from creating a movement." Word of this simple, defiant protest quickly spread across social media. Before the end of 2018, more than twenty thousand students from around the world, in Japan, Australia, Belgium, and the United States, were following her example and choosing protest over school.

Behind that podium in Poland a few months later, Greta's task was to spell out the truth of climate change in such a way as to prevent her adult audience from dismissing it yet again. No small challenge, as most of the world's leaders had been disregarding the urgent pleas of the scientific community for quite some time.

Greta spoke with an unadorned frankness that was impossible to ignore. "We have to speak clearly, no matter how uncomfortable that may be," she said. The uncomfortable truth she had come to name included this bold claim: "Our civilization is being sacrificed for the opportunity of a very small number of people to continue making enormous amounts of money."

Greta didn't merely hold firm to her truth; she demonstrated a willingness for confrontation by directly accusing her audience of failing to act. Indeed, rather than be intimidated by the fact that she was a child speaking at a conference full of adults, Greta actually drew attention to the age disparity, using it to her advantage: "You are not mature enough to tell it like it is," she said, "even that burden you leave to us children . . . You say you love your children above all else, and yet you are stealing their future in front of their very eyes."

The fight against global warming is importantly different from the other movements covered in these pages. All those causes grew out of an effort to address an injustice that was already present in people's lives: the injustice of gender discrimination, the injustice of worker exploitation, the injustice of totalitarianism.

Though we're already seeing the first effects of global warming, in many senses this is an injustice the present is inflicting on the future, that adults are forcing on today's youth and children yet to be born. Our desire to enjoy today the levels of consumption we've grown used to is coming at the expense of those who will inhabit our planet tomorrow.

This aspect of the truth about climate change gives Greta Thunberg and thousands of other young people a special authority when they choose to speak out and act out, which may explain the sudden potency of their protest. As Bill McKibben, a longtime climate change activist, put it, "The movement that Greta launched is one of the most hopeful things in my thirty years of working on the climate question. It throws the generational challenge of global warming into its sharpest relief, and challenges adults to prove they are, actually, adults."

As McKibben notes, the climate change movement is nothing new. Experts have been warning about the dangers of global warming for decades.

In this regard, like Alice Paul was for suffrage, so Greta Thunberg is for demanding action on climate change: a new activist joining an old movement, an idealistic radical unfazed by widespread apathy, a single-minded satyagrahi indifferent to the supposed "reality" of what most everyone else assumes is and isn't possible. Greta knows that a generation or two of the world's adult leaders have failed to heed the warnings; she knows that other activists, grown-up activists no less passionate than she, have been ignored for years.

Greta doesn't care.

Greta Thunberg is on the autism spectrum and describes herself on her Twitter page as a "climate activist with Asperger." She believes that this condition, which some might see as a disadvantage, is actually central to her ability, and even need, to advocate for action so relentlessly:

> For those of us on the spectrum, almost everything is black or white. We aren't very good at lying and we usually don't enjoy participating in the social game as the rest of you seem so fond of. I think in many ways we autistic are the normal ones and the rest of the people are pretty strange—especially when it comes to the sustainability crisis.

Properly responding to the dangers of global warming will require wide-scale institutional changes. Everything from how we get around to how we grow our food to how we keep our homes warm at night will have to be rethought and reworked. But the failure of our current political leadership to take serious action suggests that in this case institutional activism won't be enough to create the necessary change, especially considering how quickly this change must come.

Hence the nonviolent direct action of Greta Thunberg and all the other young people who have chosen to follow her example. As she puts it: "Some say that we should not engage in activism. Instead we should leave everything to our politicians and just vote for changes. But what do we do when there is no political will? What do we do when the politics needed are nowhere in sight?"

And a school strike is the perfect type of civil disobedience for a young person to engage in when it comes to drawing attention to climate change. Nothing demonstrates the power adults have over children better than the fact that day after day kids agree to show up in class at all. But, as Greta says, "Why should any young person be made to study for a future when no one is doing enough to save that future? What is the point of learning facts when the most important facts given by the finest scientists are ignored by our politicians?"

We study history for different reasons. Sometimes it is a matter of simple curiosity: How did that skinny, bald Indian man dressed in only sandals and a white sheet lead an entire nation to independence? Sometimes the stories are just too unbelievable to pass up: Want to hear the one about the playwright who helped topple a repressive regime and then became his country's president?

But those of us who stick with history ultimately do it for another, deeper reason: we believe we have a responsibility to know about the past, because the better we understand it, the better we'll know how to act in the present.

Each of the chapters in this book describes people who responded responsibly, courageously, and defiantly to the injustices of their day. These activists saw something in their society that needed to be fixed and decided they couldn't just hope for someone else to come along and fix it. They believed that even though the seemingly powerful preferred things to remain just the way they were, that if enough regular people banded together to demand change that change would eventually come.

Oftentimes it was the young who fueled these nonviolent movements. In 1989, students in Prague marched at the head of a demonstration that turned into a massacre that quickly freed their country. The Children's Crusade in Birmingham, Alabama, in which children as young as six skipped school to confront fire hoses and dogs and long nights in jail, is now seen

by many as the decisive battle of the entire civil rights movement.

Maybe the climate change movement will prove the power of young people once more. In the United States, youth leadership is taking Greta's example seriously. US Youth Climate Strike—an organization led by teens as young as thirteen-year-old Haven Coleman—seeks to replicate Thunberg's school strikes and is currently active in over forty states. The even

Hope Is Contagious. Less than a year after striking from school all alone, Greta Thunberg (marching here above the S in HOUSE) was part of a global nonviolent movement with well over a million activists.

larger Sunrise Movement—led by twenty-five-year-old Varshini Prakash—aims for institutional change: getting the Democratic Party to support meaningful action on climate change. But they use disruptive nonviolent action to draw attention to the urgency of their message. Following the 2018 midterm elections, Sunrise Movement organized sit-ins of congressional offices to demand that their representatives take real steps to ween the country off of fossil fuels.

These activists have begun speaking their truths and they have shown their willingness to make things uncomfortable for those who prefer not to be bothered at all. On March 15, 2019, barely half a year since Thunberg began striking by herself, 1.4 million mostly young protesters in more than one hundred countries around the world, having "done our homework" when it comes to the truth of climate change, joined Greta's school strike. It was the biggest single day of climate activism in history.

All these people came together not merely in response to the truth of climate change. There is another truth these young protesters know, a truth that inspired them to leave the classroom for the streets in the first place, a fundamental truth that Greta concluded with back behind that podium in Poland:

> We have not come here to beg world leaders to care. You have ignored us in the past and you will ignore us again. We have run out of excuses and we are running out of time. We have come here to let you know that change is coming whether you like it or not–the real power belongs to the people.

It's easy to succumb to despair when thinking about the future of climate change, but there is reason for hope: the power of these young activists has already begun to transform mainstream politics. By spring 2019, a clear majority of the candidates vying to become the Democratic presidential candidate were supporting the Green New Deal, a wide-ranging, ambitious program to address climate change. Meanwhile the governments of Ireland, Scotland, Canada, and England have all declared a climate emergency in order to acknowledge the severity of the situation and begin the society-wide mobilization that will be required to address it. Other nations are sure to follow. As more and more people confront the truth about climate change and recognize the need for a massive, coordinated plan to address it, the politicians representing them will have little choice but to respond in kind.

The lesson from all this is as simple as it is inspiring, and it's a lesson that extends well beyond the classroom.

Greta Thunberg sums it up best: "Activism works. So act."

POSTSCRIPT

On August 28, 2019, near the end of a summer that saw two of the hottest months on record, Greta Thunberg arrived in New York. She had traveled—by sailing for fifteen days aboard a zero-emissions racing yacht—to the most powerful country on earth to spread her truth and call for action.

And the people listened.

On September 20, barely a year after Greta began striking alone, approximately 4 million people in over 160 countries around the world took to the streets once again to sound the alarm for climate change. This time, adult workers joined the strikes, leaving their jobs to lift up the voices of the young people leading the way.

According to Dr. Erica Chenoweth, an expert on nonviolent resistance, there's something called the "3.5% rule." Since 1900 no nonviolent campaign has failed after securing the "active and sustained participation of just 3.5% of the population."

In the United States, this means 11 million people. For a global movement, 3.5% would require the mobilization of over 250 million people. It might sound like a lot, but after growing from a single person to 7 million in only a year, nothing is out of reach.

And every person counts. Including you.

A Growing Global Movement. Youth activists in Chicago lead one of the 4,500 climate protests that took place around the world between September 20 and September 27, 2019.

Other Notable Nonviolent Movements of the Last One Hundred Years

THE LAST ONE HUNDRED YEARS HAVE SEEN AN EXTRAORdinary surge in nonviolent movements all around the globe. In fact, the incredible people in these pages represent just a fraction of the countless activists who have changed the world with their courage, vision, and determination. If you're interested in learning about other movements, here's a list to get you started.

Denmark's Noncooperation Thwarts Nazi Germany and Saves Thousands

Skeptics often argue that nonviolence could never work when dealing with a ruthless, powerful adversary. But the case of Danish resistance to the Nazi occupation during World War II shows otherwise. By regularly striking in factories and rail yards, the Danish masses prevented Germany from exploiting their country's labor, resources, and infrastructure. This resistance was coordinated by the Danish Freedom Council, an underground government, and embodied by monarch King Christian, who rode his horse daily through the streets of Copenhagen to express Danish pride and independence. When German forces attempted to round up Denmark's eight thousand Jews, regular Danes warned them, hid them, and eventually helped the vast majority of them to escape safely to neutral Sweden.

ACT UP Draws Attention to the AIDS Epidemic and Forces Government Action

In the late 1980s, AIDS was spreading quickly. Tens of thousands of people, many of them gay men, had already been infected by this new disease, which looked to be little more than a death sentence. Despite the danger posed by AIDS, President Ronald Reagan barely mentioned its name, the government invested next to nothing in medical research to fight it, and the most promising drugs available to treat it were outrageously expensive. But in 1987 a new organization, ACT UP, emerged to challenge this lethal state of affairs. Seeking confrontation and disruption in order to bring attention to the plight of those infected, these desperate, determined activists tried everything, from lying down with cardboard tombstones on Broadway in New

York City to chaining themselves inside the offices of drug companies. ACT UP transformed public opinion about AIDS and forced those in power to treat the epidemic for what it was, saving thousands of lives in the process.

Ending Apartheid and Enabling Reconciliation in South Africa

Starting in 1912, black South Africans fought to overturn the racist system, eventually called apartheid, that the minority white population created to control the country. For decades the majority black population adhered to nonviolent methods, but their struggle grew violent in the 1950s, leading to much bloodshed and the imprisonment of its leadership. After abandoning armed struggle in the 1980s, activists employed a vast array of tactics—including boycotts, strikes, and protests—to convince the white leadership that the time to reject apartheid had finally arrived. This return to nonviolence prevented a violent civil war, enabled a peaceful transfer of power in 1994, and ultimately made it possible for the entire country to confront, nonviolently, its oppressive past through the creation of the Truth and Reconciliation Commission.

Liberian Women End Their Country's Civil War

In 2003, Liberia's second civil war was three years old and had already claimed more than 200,000 lives. A group of women, led by Leymah Gbowee, joined together to demand that the government and warlords meet to end the fighting. Using sit-ins, protests, vigils, marches, and even their refusal to have physical relations with their partners, these women eventually pressured President Charles Taylor to hold peace talks, which Gbowee and fellow activists attended in order to ensure progress was made. The war ended later that year, but the women's organization remained active until 2005, when democratic elections brought Ellen Johnson Sirleaf, the country's first female president, into power.

Occupy Wall Street and the Rise of the 99%

On September 17, 2011, a couple hundred protesters occupied Zuccotti Park, located just blocks from Wall Street and the New York Stock Exchange. The protesters' slogan, "We are the ninety-nine percent," drew attention to the pressing problems of income and wealth inequality in the United States, where the top 1 percent makes 25 percent of the nation's income and owns 40 percent of its overall wealth. The protesters, sleeping in tents, lived in the park for almost two months before being driven out in mid-November. Though some argue that Occupy Wall Street was a failure, since in the short-term the protesters achieved none of their goals, this movement transformed how Americans view wealth and inequality. In 2016, Bernie Sanders, once considered a marginal member of the Senate, ran on a platform echoing Occupy's concerns and nearly won the Democratic nomination for president.

Black Lives Matter Protests Against Police Brutality

On May 25, 2020, a Minneapolis policeman killed George Floyd, an unarmed Black man, in broad daylight. The murder was caught on video and protests quickly spread across the country. In many places, the police violently suppressed peaceful demonstrations. This use of force backfired against the authorities by illustrating the protestors' claim that police brutality is rampant in the United States. Some protests eventually grew violent, with looting and destruction of property occurring in several major cities. These incidents were the exception, however, and in June 2020 at least fifteen million Americans participated in nonviolent protests that took place in over two thousand communities scattered across every state in the nation. This ongoing movement has already led to police reform at the state and federal level while bringing awareness to the stubborn problem of institutionalized racism.

And the Story Continues . . .

As of this writing, the future of the decentralized Black Lives Matters movement—including its tactics—remains uncertain. But one thing is clear: Despite the restrictions imposed on everyone during the COVID-19 pandemic, nonviolent activism is alive and well, and not just in the United States. Around the world, regular people are coming together to claim power in places as varied as Hong Kong, Algeria, and Belarus.

It's too soon to know if these recent flare-ups will develop into movements capable of forever altering their countries' political landscapes. But one thing is sure: As more and more individuals learn about nonviolent activism, and as more and more people study its past successes as a blueprint for today, more and more activists will come to see the boundless potential of nonviolence to transform their communities, countries, and our world as a whole.

NOTES

Chapter 1: Gandhi and Indian Independence

2 "I regard myself as a soldier . . .": Paul K. Chappell, *Peaceful Revolution: How We Can Create the Future Needed for Humanity's Survival.* Westport, CT: Easton Studio Press, 2012, 174.

3 "I shuddered as I read the sections . . .": M. K. Gandhi, *Satyagraha in South Africa* Ahmedabad, India: Navajivan Publishing House, 1972, 99.

4 "We may have to go to jail . . .": ibid., 106–107.

8 "respect our own language, speak it well . . .": Ramachandra Guha, *Gandhi Before India* New York, NY: Alfred A. Knopf, 2014, 262.

8 "internal violence": Dennis Dalton, *Mahatma Gandhi: Nonviolent Power in Action.* New York, NY: Columbia University Press, 1993, 38.

9 "Satya . . . truth . . . agraha . . . holding firmly": ibid, 9.

9 "truth force": ibid, 38.

9 "soul force": Jonathan Schell, *The Unconquerable World: Power, Nonviolence, and the Will of the People.* New York, NY: Metropolitan Books, 2003, 130.

9 "born of Truth and Love or nonviolence": Dalton, *Mahatma Gandhi*, 8.

10 "the sword of satyagraha": Guha, *Gandhi Before India*, 279.

10 "'love' . . . 'noninjury'": Dalton, *Mahatma Gandhi*, 14; and Rufus Burrow Jr., *Extremist for Love: Martin Luther King, Jr., Man of Ideas and Nonviolent Social Action.* Minneapolis, MN: Fortress Press, 2014, 231.

11 "Our whole struggle is based on our submitting ourselves . . .": Guha, *Gandhi Before India*, 251.

12 "sent every leader to prison, and hundreds more . . .": ibid, 271.

12 "not crow over their victory": David Hardiman, *The Nonviolent Struggle for Indian Freedom, 1905–1919*. London, UK: Hurst Publishers, 2018) 85.

15 "in any great war, more than one battle . . .": M. K. Gandhi, *The Collected Works of Mahatma Gandhi*. New Delhi, India: Government of India, 1958, vol. 8, 404.

15 "Kaffir": Guha, *Gandhi Before India*, 181.

16 "The crowd hurrahed and shouted themselves hoarse . . .": Gandhi, *The Collected Works*, vol. 8, 456.

16 "dead letter": ibid, 470.

17 "A more reliable and more honorable method . . .": Guha, *Gandhi Before India*, 254.

18 "India itself, the idea that women . . .": ibid, 464–465.

18 "were not supposed to leave . . .": ibid, 465.

19 "vanguard": ibid, 467.

21 "only fair means can produce . . .": ibid, 368.

21 "The saint has left our shores . . .": Judith M. Brown, *Gandhi: Prisoner of Hope*. New Haven, CT: Yale University Press, 1991, 74.

21 "perhaps the mightiest instrument on earth": Guha, *Gandhi Before India*, 550.

24 "inner voice": Dalton, *Mahatma Gandhi*, 98.

24 "four times as expensive as in England": Ramachandra Guha, *Gandhi: The Years That Changed the World, 1914–1948*. New York, NY: Alfred A. Knopf, 2018, 318.

25 "Next to air and water . . .": Dalton, *Mahatma Gandhi*, 100.

25 "Dear friend . . . Before embarking . . .": for full text of Gandhi's letter, see sites.google.com/site/mgandhithesaltmarch/letter-to-lord-irwin.

27 "regrettably hale and hearty": Brown, *Prisoner of Hope*, 238.

27 "The English have not taken India . . .": Mohandas K. Gandhi, *Hind Swaraj*. New Delhi, India: Rajpal & Sons, 2011, 31.

29 "To arrest Gandhi is to court a war . . .": Dalton, *Mahatma Gandhi*, 112.

30 "I want world sympathy in this battle . . .": ibid, 114.

31 "lumps of natural salt lying in a small pit . . .": Guha, *The Years That Changed the World*, 331.

31 "Hail, law breaker": ibid, 331.

31 "It seemed as though a spring . . .": Joan Bondurant, *Conquest of Violence: The Gandhian Philosophy of Conflict*. Princeton, NJ: Princeton University Press, 1988, 94.

35 "Nonviolence is the greatest force . . .": Anand Sharma, ed. *Gandhian Way: Peace, Nonviolence, and Empowerment*. New Delhi, India: Academic Foundation, 2007, 23.

Chapter 2: Alice Paul and Votes for Women

38 "History had taught us that no great reform . . .": Dawn Keetley and John Pettegrew, eds., *Public Women, Public Words: A Documentary History of American Feminism*. Lanham, MD: Rowman & Littlefield, 2002, 211.

40 "women could not undertake the physical responsibilities . . .": Susan K. Kent, *Sex and Suffrage in Britain 1860–1914*. London, UK: Routledge, 1990, 184.

40 "the time has come . . .": Mary Chapman, *Making Noise, Making News: Suffrage Print Culture and U.S. Modernism*. New York, NY: Oxford University Press, 2017, 77.

42 "erratic heart": J. D. Zahniser and Amelia R. Fry, *Alice Paul: Claiming Power*. New York, NY: Oxford University Press, 2014, 251.

43 "How long, how long . . .": Tina Cassidy, *Mr. President, How Long Must We Wait? Alice Paul, Woodrow Wilson, and the Fight for the Right to Vote*. New York, NY: 37 INK/Atria Books, 2019, 133.

43 "As the leader of a Party . . .": Doris Stevens, *Jailed for Freedom: American Women Win the Vote*. Troutdale, OR: NewSage Press, 1995.

44 "We have got to take a new departure . . .": Zahniser and Fry, *Alice Paul*, 255.

46 "General Orders . . . Commandant . . . Officer of the Day . . . Privates . . . Morning Detail . . . Sergeant of the Guard": Mary Walton, *A Woman's Crusade: Alice Paul and the Battle for the Ballot*. New York, NY: St. Martin's Griffin, 2010, 148.

48 "every known scientific device . . . was a BANNER!": Bernadette Cahill, *Alice Paul, the National Woman's Party, and the First Civil Rights Struggle of the 20th Century*. Jefferson, NC: McFarland & Company, Inc., 2015, 81.

49 "sang, yelled, whistled . . . from beginning to end": Zahniser and Fry, *Alice Paul*, 46.

50 "Deeds, not Words": ibid, 66.

50 "papier-mache armor . . . ropes of spinners' cotton wool": ibid, 69.

51 "awful scene . . . a wonder that no one was killed . . . on their backs over & over again": ibid, 70.

52 "One of the doctors stood . . .": ibid, 99.

54 "Just a little stone in a big mosaic": ibid, 104.

55 "testimony . . . valiant for the Truth upon earth": Katherine H. Adams and Michael L. Keene, *Alice Paul and the American*

Suffrage Campaign. Urbana and Chicago, IL: University of Illinois Press, 2008, 3.

55 "process of Moral evolution": ibid, 31.

56 "It is not militant in the sense . . .": ibid, 32.

56 "did not come to make peace . . . came to fight": Peter Ackerman and Jack Duvall, *A Force More Powerful: A Century of Nonviolent Conflict*. New York, NY: St. Martin's Press, 2000, 5.

58 "There is no Alice Paul . . . She leads by being . . .": Christine Lunardini, *Alice Paul: Equality for Women*. Boulder, CO: Westview Press, 2012, 9.

58 "Miss Paul neither eats . . . the Federal Amendment": Adams and Keene, *Alice Paul*, 34.

59 "Where are the people . . . watching the suffrage parade": Jean H. Baker, *Sisters: The Lives of America's Suffragists*. New York, NY: Hill and Wang, 2006, 184.

61 "to march steadily in a dignified manner": ibid.

61 "never heard such vulgar . . . language": Cahill, *Alice Paul*, 58.

62 "It was meant to happen . . . only to be determined about it": Walton, *Woman's Crusade*, 79.

62 "catastrophe, but an unlooked-for blessing . . . public indignation and sympathy": ibid.

63 "'Police Must Face Charges . . . little less than riots,'": Walton, *Woman's Crusade*, 78.

64 "the paramount issue of the day": Zahniser and Fry, *Alice Paul*, 164.

64 "But Mr. President . . . without first getting the consent of women": Walton, *Woman's Crusade*, 83.

66 "It seemed to us only fair . . .": Zahniser and Fry, *Alice Paul*, 265.

67 "President Wilson and Envoy Root . . ."; Baker, *Sisters*, 216.

68 "countered her instincts . . . not an offender in any way": Walton, *Woman's Crusade*, 176.

69 "Why has picketing suddenly . . .": Baker, *Sisters*, 216.

69 "The picketing will go on . . .": Cassidy, *Mr. President*, 162.

70 "Them's the President's own . . .": Deborah Kops, *Alice Paul and the Fight for Women's Rights: From the Vote to the Equal Rights Amendment*. Honesdale, PA: Calkins Creek, 2017, 89.

71 "Not a dollar of your fine . . .": Eleanor Clift, *Founding Sisters and the Nineteenth Amendment*. Hoboken, NJ: John Wiley & Sons, 2003, 131.

71 "We know full well . . .": Stevens, *Jailed for Freedom*, 80.

72 "The next lot of women . . .": Walton, *Woman's Crusade*, 186.

73 "KAISER WILSON have you . . .": Stevens, *Jailed for Freedom*, 88.

76 "I shall *never* go . . .": Walton, *Woman's Crusade*, 27.

77 "I will show you . . .": ibid, 195.

77 "I believe I have never . . .": Stevens, *Jailed for Freedom*, 118.

78 "such numbers that the government . . .": Walton, *Woman's Crusade*, 194.

80 "blazing little eyes": ibid, 197.

80 "Shut up. Sit down.": Winifred Conkling, *Votes for Women! American Suffragists and the Battle for the Ballot*. New York, NY: Algonquin Young Readers, 2018, 247.

81 "depend upon the attitude the Administration . . .": Inez Haynes Gillmore, *The Story of the Woman's Party*. London, UK: Forgotten Books, 2019, 255.

82 "the easiest thing in the world . . . treat you as political prisoners.": Adams and Keene, *Alice Paul*, 198.

82 "make it known to the leaders . . .": Gillmore, *The Story*, 255.

83 "We are put out of jail . . .": Baker, *Sisters*, 220.

83 "political jiujitsu": Lee A. Smithey and Lester R. Kurtz, eds., *The Paradox of Repression of Nonviolent Movements*. Syracuse, NY: Syracuse University Press, 2018, xvi.

84 "We hope that no more demonstrations . . .": Zahniser and Fry, *Alice Paul*, 296.

86 "Paul was trying to alter . . .": Adams and Keene, *Alice Paul*, 36.

Chapter 3: Martin Luther King Jr. and Project C

90 "The only weapon we have . . .": Martin Luther King, Jr., Montgomery Bus Boycott Speech, December 5, 1955. Full audio and text at www.youtube.com/watch?time_continue=34&v=GGtp7kCi_LA.

90 "Listen, nigger . . . we've taken . . .": Martin Luther King, Jr., *Stride Toward Freedom: The Montgomery Story*. Boston, MA: Beacon Press, 2010, 124.

92 "I am afraid . . .": ibid, 125.

92 "Stand up for righteousness . . .": ibid, 125.

93 "I have not come to bring peace . . .": ibid, 27.

96 "If you have weapons, take them home . . .": Taylor Branch, *Parting the Waters: America in the King Years 1954–1963* New York, NY: Simon & Schuster, 1989, 166.

99 "not a single racial barrier fell": Mark Engler and Paul Engler, *This Is an Uprising: How Nonviolent Revolt Is Shaping the Twenty-First Century*. New York, NY: Bold Type Books, 2017, vii.

100 "Birmingham is where it's at . . .": Henry Hampton and Steve Fayer with Sarah Flynn, *Voices of Freedom: An Oral History*

of the Civil rights movement from the 1950s through the 1980s. New York, NY: Bantam, 1991, 125.

101 Dynamite Hill . . . Bombingham: Diane McWhorter, *Carry Me Home: Birmingham, Alabama: The Climactic Battle of the Civil Rights Revolution.* New York, NY: Simon & Schuster, 2001, 2, 57.

101 "by far the worst big city in the US . . .": Branch, *Parting the Waters*, 684.

101 Project C . . . "confrontation": Engler and Engler, *This Is an Uprising*, viii.

102 "cripple the city . . ." Branch, *Parting the Waters*, 689.

102 "a situation so crisis-packed . . . pus-flowing ugliness": Engler and Engler, *This Is an Uprising*, ix.

103 "There are eleven people here . . .": Branch, *Parting the Waters*, 691–692.

104 "B-Day," Sean Chabot, *Transnational Roots of the Civil rights movement: African American Explorations of the Ghandian Repertoire.* Lanham, MD: Rowman & Littlefield, 2013, 162.

104 "We're tired of waiting . . .": Cynthia Levinson, *We've Got a Job: The 1963 Birmingham Children's March.* Atlanta, GA: Peachtree Publishers, 2012, 56.

105 "our most dedicated and devoted . . .": Branch, *Parting the Waters*, 729.

105 "faith act": ibid.

105 "the hole": ibid, 731.

106 "unwise and untimely": ibid, 737.

106 "universal voice, beyond time . . .": ibid, 740.

106 "Injustice anywhere is a threat . . .": Jonathan Rieder, *Gospel of Freedom: Martin Luther King, Jr.'s Letter from Birmingham*

Jail and the Struggle That Changed a Nation. New York, NY: Bloomsbury Press, 2014, 170.

106 "The time is always ripe . . .": ibid, 178.

106 "Oppressed people cannot . . .": ibid, 164.

107 "King's letter from a silent cry . . .": Branch, *Parting the Waters*, 744.

108 "I consider myself a rabbi": McWhorter, *Carry Me Home*, 291.

109 "spiritual kamikaze": Branch, *Parting the Waters*, 735.

109 "Birmingham is sick": Levinson, *We've Got a Job*, 59.

109 "Some Negroes don't want . . .": McWhorter, *Carry Me Home*, 337.

109 "white trash": Glenn T. Eskew, *But for Birmingham: The Local and National Movements in the Civil Rights Struggle.* Chapel Hill, NC: The University of North Carolina Press, 1997, 242.

109 "You can put me in jail . . .": Levinson, *We've Got a Job*, 59.

109 "The police can come to our meeting . . .": ibid.

110 "Some of these students say . . .": Eskew, *But for Birmingham*, 242–243.

110 "You are responsible for segregation . . .": Hampton and Fayer, *Voices of Freedom*, 131–132.

111 "No comment": Levinson, *We've Got a Job*, 33.

111 "REFRAIN from the violence of fist . . .": ibid, 34.

112 "This was a nonviolent academy . . .": ibid, 34–35.

112 whisper campaign: McWhorter, *Carry Me Home*, 343.

112 "In forty years you are going to be here . . .": ibid.

113 "conscious acceptance": Branch, *Parting the Waters*, 755.

114 "We got to use what . . .": McWhorter, *Carry Me Home*, 345.

114 "Meatball": Levinson, *We've Got a Job*, 69.

114 "We are going to break Birmingham . . .": ibid.

114 "D-Day": McWhorter, *Carry Me Home*, 348.

115 "Kids, there's gonna be a party . . . lunch will be served": ibid.

115 "hayride . . . sock hop": Levinson, *We've Got a Job*, 72.

116 "I'll Die to Make . . . Hate His Brother": ibid, 74.

118 "Hey, Fred . . . God Almighty": McWhorter, *Carry Me Home*, 349.

119 "Six": Branch, *Parting the Waters*, 757.

119 "The whole world is watching . . .": ibid.

119 "If they think today . . ." Levinson, *We've Got a Job*, 77.

120 "Double D-Day": ibid, 81.

121 "monitor guns": Branch, *Parting the Waters*, 759.

121 "or you're going to get wet": ibid, 758.

121 "The pressure from that hose . . .": Levinson, *We've Got a Job*, 82.

122 "outside agitators": McWhorter, *Carry Me Home*, 4.

122 "Lawyer Vann . . .": ibid, 353.

123 "Stop the car now": Shelley Tougas, *Birmingham 1963: How a Photograph Rallied Civil Rights Support*. Mankato, MN: Compass Point Books, 2011, 33.

123 "Bring the dogs": McWhorter, *Carry Me Home*, 353.

125 "Your daughters and sons are in jail . . .": Levinson, *We've Got a Job*, 89.

125 "We have a nonviolent movement . . .": Branch, *Parting the Waters*, 763.

127 "television's greatest hour": McWhorter, *Carry Me Home*, 356.

128 "It was a masterpiece . . .": Hampton and Fayer, *Voices of Freedom*, 133.

128 "sick": Branch, *Parting the Waters*, 764.

129 "We're tired of this mess . . .": ibid, 766.

129 "We're not turning back . . .": McWhorter, *Carry Me Home*, 369.

130 "Turn on your water . . .": Branch, *Parting the Waters*, 767.

130 "Dammit! Turn on the hoses!": Levinson, *We've Got a Job*, 109.

130 "You turn it on yourself . . .": ibid.

130 "We're here to put out fires . . .": McWhorter, *Carry Me Home*, 369.

130 "Let us proceed": Branch, *Parting the Waters*, 768.

131 "Once you arrest three thousand people . . .": Levinson, *We've Got a Job*, 118.

131 "sign a paper saying . . .": Branch, *Parting the Waters*, 780.

132 "white and black": Levinson, *We've Got a Job*, 127.

134 "That's the motel": McWhorter, *Carry Me Home*, 411.

135 "Our *home* was just bombed . . .": Branch, *Parting the Waters*, 795.

135 "We don't need any guns . . . it'll kill somebody": Levinson, *We've Got a Job*, 133.

136 "the 'thonk' of clubs . . .": Branch, *Parting the Waters*, 796.

138 "I hope that every American . . . content to have the color . . . This nation, for all its hopes . . . race has no place in American life or law": Jolyon P. Girard, Darryl Mace, and Courtney Michelle Smith, eds., *American History through its Greatest Speeches: A Documentary History of the United States*. Santa Barbara, CA: ABC-CLIO, 2017, 181–182.

139 "We must forever conduct . . .": Gary Younge, *The Speech: The Story Behind Dr. Martin Luther King Jr.'s Dream*. Chicago, IL: Haymarket Books, 2013, xiii.

Chapter 4: Cesar Chavez and the Farmworkers' Movement

144 "Once social change begins . . .": Jose-Antonio Orosco, *Cesar Chavez and the Common Sense of Nonviolence*. Albuquerque, NM: University of New Mexico Press, 2008, 23.

147 "just another item in producing products . . .": Lionel Steinberg, quoted in the documentary, *The Struggle in the Fields*. 3:25, www.youtube.com/watch?time_continue=2&v=gz-OclhZpEI.

147 "a shocking degree of human misery . . .": Randy Shaw, *Beyond the Fields: Cesar Chavez, the UFW, and the Struggle for Justice in the 21st Century*. Berkeley, CA: University of California Press, 2008, 15.

148 "reject a culture which . . .": Orosco, *Cesar Chavez*, 24.

149 "Fred did such a good job . . .": Jacques E. Levy, *Cesar Chavez: Autobiography of La Causa*. Minneapolis, MN: University of Minnesota Press, 2007, 99.

149 "I think I've found the guy . . .": ibid, 102.

150 "potholes to police brutality": Susan Ferriss and Ricardo Sandoval, *The Fight in the Fields: Cesar Chavez and the Farmworkers Movement*. New York, NY: Harcourt Brace & Company, 1997, 6.

151 "It's true, they're powerful . . . their power to make it go": Levy, *Cesar Chavez*, xxix.

153 "If in six months we don't . . .": ibid, 165.

153 "The harder a guy is . . .": Ferriss and Sandoval, *The Fight in the Fields*, 68.

155 "He was organizing us": ibid, 69.

156 "Black was for the workers' desperation . . .": Miriam Pawel, *The Crusades of Cesar Chavez*. New York: Bloomsbury Press, 2014, 89.

157 "You are here to discuss . . .": Richard G. Del Castilla and Richard A. Garcia, *Cesar Chavez: A Triumph of Spirit*. Norman, OK: University of Oklahoma Press, 1995, 43–44.

158 "Huelga, huelga, huelga!": Pawel, *The Crusades*, 104.

159 "Oh God . . .": ibid, 105.

160 "But it must not be . . .": Ferriss and Sandoval, *The Fight in the Fields*, 89.

161 "nonviolent army": Orosco, *Cesar Chavez*, 24.

161 "Are you in agreement . . . Sí!": Levy, *Cesar Chavez*, 185.

163 "If we can keep our great strike . . .": Pawel, *The Crusades*, 107.

163 "They have the money . . .": ibid, 109.

164 "Huelga! Huelga! Huelga!": Frank Bardacke, *Trampling Out the Vintage: Cesar Chavez and the Two Souls of the United Farm Workers*. London: Verso, 2011, 172.

166 "We took every case of violence . . .": Ferriss and Sandoval, *The Fight in the Fields*, 97.

167 "Don't eat grapes . . . Is this a labor dispute . . . Come with me . . . He got on his hands . . .": Marshall Ganz, *Why David Sometimes Wins: Leadership, Organization, and Strategy in the California Farm Worker Movement*. New York, NY: Oxford University Press, 2009, 140–141.

168 "secondary boycotts": Bardacke, *Trampling Out*, 176.

172 "We'll stay here . . .": Levy, *Cesar Chavez*, 208.

172 "We are tired of words . . .": Pawel, *The Crusades*, 126.

173 "worn-out low shoes . . . like a melon . . . left foot was just . . .": Levy, *Cesar Chavez*, 211.

173 "Some people had bloody feet . . .": Bardacke, *Trampling Out*, 235.

174 "with a mixture of bafflement . . .": Pawel, *The Crusades*, 128.

174 "The simple truth is . . .": ibid.

175 "DiGiorgio" may also be found in accounts spelled as "Di Giorgio." Spelling it as one word is based on the books of Miriam Pawel, who wrote several authoritative books on the farmworkers' movement, one of which is listed in the bibliography.

175 "call a special session . . .": Ferriss and Sandoval, *The Fight in the Fields*, 123.

178 "making plans for what to do . . .": ibid, 132.

178 "Everyone just exploded . . . People were jumping up . . .": ibid.

178 "I extend the hand of fellowship . . .": ibid, 133.

179 "If we can crack Giumarra . . .": ibid, 138.

180 "single-mindedly, day and night": Pawel, *The Crusades*, 185.

180 "Do not even entertain . . . He told them they . . .": ibid.

180 "Don't eat grapes": Gabriel Thompson, *America's Social Arsonist: Fred Ross and Grassroots Organizing in the Twentieth Century*. Berkeley, CA: University of California Press, 2016, 193.

181 "Please don't shop . . .": Pawel, *The Crusades*, 186.

182 "Where's Chicago?": Ferriss and Sandoval, *The Fight in the Fields*, 139.

182 "Hi, I'm a farmworker . . .": Miriam Pawel, "Former Chavez Ally Took His Own Path," *Los Angeles Times*, February 15, 2006.

182 "This is my chance . . . To be truthful . . .": Ferriss and Sandoval, *The Fight in the Fields*, 146–147.

184 "You can't do business . . .": Pawel, *The Crusades*, 189.

185 "Priests sat in produce aisles . . .": ibid, 186.

186 "What we're asking you . . .": Shaw, *Beyond the Fields*, 30.

187 "We just totally disrupted . . ." Ferriss and Sandoval, *The Fight in the Fields*, 153.

188 "Millions of pounds of grapes . . ." Griswold and Garcia, *Cesar Chavez*, 91.

188 "the biggest, most successful . . .": Bardacke, *Trampling Out*, 164.

189 "wearing an immaculate . . .": Ferriss and Sandoval, *The Fight in the Fields*, 157.

189 "If it works well here . . .": ibid.

190 "Without the help of . . ." Pawel, *The Crusades*, 208–209.

Chapter 5: Václav Havel and the Velvet Revolution

194 "If the main pillar of the system . . .": Václav Havel, *Open Letters: Selected Writings 1965–1990*. New York, NY: Alfred A. Knopf, 1991, 148.

196 "Free Elections . . . Democracy and Law . . . if not now": Bernard Wheaton and Zdenek Kavan, *Velvet Revolution: Czechoslovakia, 1988–1991*. Boulder, CO: Westview Press, 1992, 42.

196 "Today we shall not just . . .": Krapfl, James, *Revolution with a Human Face: Politics, Culture, and Community in Czechoslovakia, 1989–1992*. Ithaca, NY: Cornell University Press, 2013, 46.

198 "We don't want violence": Wheaton and Kavan, *Velvet Revolution*, 44.

198 "We have empty hands": Krapfl, *Revolution*, 47.

198 living altar: ibid.

199 "the massacre": ibid, 14.

200 "socialism with a human face": Paulina Bren, *The Greengrocer and His TV: The Culture of Communism After the 1968 Prague Spring*. Ithaca, NY: Cornell University Press, 2010, 59.

202 "Whenever you meet members . . .": Gene Sharp, *Waging Nonviolent Struggle: 20th Century Practice and 21st Century Potential*. Boston, MA: Extending Horizons Books, 2005, 191.

202 "Let your weapon be . . .": ibid, 192.

203 "Soldiers, go home!": ibid, 194.

203 "Moscow—1500 kilometers": ibid, 198.

204 "dignified counterpart . . .": Gale Stokes, *The Walls Came Tumbling Down: Collapse and Rebirth in Eastern Europe*. New York, NY: Oxford University Press, 2012, 17.

205 "The fun was definitely over": ibid, 15.

205 "normalization . . . process of civilized violence": ibid, 76.

206 "Interrogations, house searches . . .": Wheaton and Kavan, *Velvet Revolution*, 8.

206 "There is just one road open . . .": Michael Zantovsky, *Havel: A Life*. New York, NY: Grove Press, 2014, 118–119.

207 "aggravated hooliganism": ibid, 165.

208 "They were simply young people . . .": Michael Long, *Making History: Czech Voices of Dissent and the Revolution of 1989*. Lanham, MD: Rowman & Littlefield, 2005, 11.

209 "hit the gas": Jonathan Bolton, *Worlds of Dissent: Charter 77, the Plastic People of the Universe, and Czech Culture under Communism*. Cambridge, MA: Harvard University Press, 2012, 149.

210 "to help enable all . . .": Long, *Making History*, 1.

211 "Workers of the world, unite!": Havel, *Open Letters*, 132.

212 "live within the truth": ibid, 146.

213 "works only as long as . . .": ibid, 141.

215 "nonviolent attempt by people . . .": ibid, 194.

215 "the prime human obligation . . .": Schell, *The Unconquerable World*, 201.

216 "A future secured by violence . . ." Havel, *Open Letters*, 184.

216 "we might not live": Zantovsky, *Havel*, 288.

219 "We were now more . . .": Jiri Sitler, Czech ambassador to Sweden, interview with author, September 29, 2018.

219 "Freedom . . . This is it . . . We have had enough!": Zantovsky, *Havel*, 303.

220 "An end to one . . . We want democracy . . . Unity is strength": Timothy G. Ash, *The Magic Lantern: The Revolution of '89 Witnessed in Warsaw, Budapest, Berlin, and Prague*. New York, NY: Random House, 1990, 123.

221 "stagehands, sound technicians . . .": Zantovsky, *Havel*, 302.

221 "amazingly loud and clear": Michael A. Kukral, *Theater of Revolution: A Study in Humantistic Political Geography*. Boulder, CO: Eastern European Monographs, 1997, 72.

223 "Havel to the Castle!": Violet B. Ketels, "'Havel to the Castle!' The Power of the Word," *The Annals of the Academy of Political and Social Science*, 542, no. 1 (1996), 52.

224 "I am a writer . . .": John K. Glenn, III, *Framing Democracy: Civil Society and Civic Movements in Eastern Europe*. Stanford, CA: Stanford University Press, 2001, 161.

224 "Those who have for many years . . .": Zantovsky, *Havel*, 303.

225 "humanness": Krapfl, *Revolution*, 7.

227 "Truth and love . . . Let us refuse any . . .": Glenn, III, *Framing Democracy*, 145.

229 "perhaps the most repressive . . .": Mark Kurlansky, *Nonviolence: The History of a Dangerous Idea.* New York, NY: Modern Library, 2008, 171.

229 "Operation Intervention": Zantovsky, *Havel*, 337.

230 "political solution to the problem . . .": Wheaton and Kavan, *Velvet Revolution*, 204.

230 "deal with the antisocialist . . .": ibid, 70.

233 "There must not be . . .": Krapfl, *Revolution*, 69.

233 "dialogue of power . . .": ibid, 19.

235 "applause turned to": ibid.

236 "Bakers, your strike is the tricolor . . .": ibid, 55.

238 "My dear fellow citizens . . .": Zantovsky, *Havel*, 331.

238 "catastrophic state": ibid.

Conclusion: Greta Thunberg and the Climate Change Movement

242 "Hope is not something that you have . . .": Emma Brockes, "When Alexandria Ocasio-Cortez Met Greta Thunberg: 'Hope is Contagious,'" *The Guardian*, June 29, 2019, www.theguardian.com/environment/2019/jun/29/alexandria-ocasio-cortez-met-greta-thunberg-hope-contagious-climate.

242 "My name is Greta Thunberg . . .": this entire speech can be found at www.youtube.com/watch?time_continue=1&v=VFkQSGyeCWg.

249 "our house is on fire": speech delivered at the World Economic Forum, January 25, 2019, www.youtube.com/watch?time_continue=1&v=M7dVF9xylaw.

249 "refused to go to school . . .": Greta Thunberg interview on Democracy Now!, December 11, 2018, www.youtube.com/watch?v=0TYyBtb1PH4.

250 "The step from one to two . . .": Greta Thunberg, "The First Time" segment with Rolling Stone, March 6, 2019, www.youtube.com/watch?v=F8g0zmDvxRw.

252 "The movement that Greta launched . . .": McKibben quoted in www.theguardian.com/environment/2019/feb/15/the-beginning-of-great-change-greta-thunberg-hails-school-climate-strikes.

253 "For those of us on the spectrum . . .": Greta Thunberg, TED Talk, November, 2018, www.ted.com/talks/greta_thunberg_school_strike_for_climate_save_the_world_by_changing_the_rules.

254 "Some say that we should not engage in activism . . .": Thunberg, World Economic Forum speech.

254 "why should any young person . . .": Greta Thunberg, "I'm striking from school to protest inaction on climate change—and you should too," *The Guardian*, November 26, 2018, amp.theguardian.com/commentisfree/2018/nov/26/im-striking-from-school-for-climate-change-too-save-the-world-australians-students-should-too.

258 "done our homework": Greta Thunberg speech to the European Economic and Social Committee, February 21, 2019, www.youtube.com/watch?v=sVeYOPJZ8oc.

259 "Activism works. So act.": Greta Thunberg tweet, May 18, 2019.

260 "active and sustained participation of just 3.5% of the population": Dr. Erica Chenoweth, rationalinsurgent.com/2013/11/04/my-talk-at-tedxboulder-civil-resistance-and-the-3-5-rule.

Bibliography

* *Suitable for young readers*

Ackerman, Peter and Jack Duvall. *A Force More Powerful: A Century of Nonviolent Conflict*. New York, NY: St. Martin's Press, 2000.

Adams, Katherine H. and Michael L. Keene. *Alice Paul and the American Suffrage Campaign*. Urbana and Chicago, IL: University of Illinois Press, 2008.

Ash, Timothy G. *The Magic Lantern: The Revolution of '89 Witnessed in Warsaw, Budapest, Berlin, and Prague*. New York, NY: Random House, 1990.

Baker, Jean H. *Sisters: The Lives of America's Suffragists*. New York, NY: Hill and Wang, 2006.

Bardacke, Frank. *Trampling Out the Vintage: Cesar Chavez and the Two Souls of the United Farm Workers*. London, UK: Verso, 2011.

Bolton, Jonathan. *Worlds of Dissent: Charter 77, the Plastic People of the Universe, and Czech Culture under Communism*. Cambridge, Mass.: Harvard University Press, 2012.

Bondurant, Joan. *Conquest of Violence: The Gandhian Philosophy of Conflict*. Princeton, NJ: Princeton University Press, 1988.

Branch, Taylor. *Parting the Waters: America in the King Years 1954–1963*. New York, NY: Simon & Schuster, 1989.

Bren, Paulina. *The Greengrocer and His TV: The Culture of Communism After the 1968 Prague Spring*. Ithaca, NY: Cornell University Press, 2010.

Brown, Judith M. *Gandhi: Prisoner of Hope*. New Haven, CT: Yale University Press, 1991.

Burns, Stewart. *To the Mountaintop: Martin Luther King Jr.'s Mission to Save America 1955–1968*. San Francisco, CA: Harper San Francisco, 2004.

Burrow Jr., Rufus. *Extremist for Love: Martin Luther King, Jr., Man of Ideas and Nonviolent Social Action*. Minneapolis, MN: Fortress Press, 2014.

Cahill, Bernadette. *Alice Paul, the National Woman's Party, and the First Civil Rights Struggle of the 20th Century*. Jefferson, NC: McFarland & Company, Inc., 2015.

Cassidy, Tina. *Mr. President, How Long Must We Wait? Alice Paul, Woodrow Wilson, and the Fight for the Right to Vote*. New York, NY: 37 INK/Atria Books, 2019.

Chabot, Sean. *Transnational Roots of the Civil rights movement: African American Explorations of the Ghandian Repertoire*. Lanham, MD: Rowman & Littlefield, 2013.

Chapman, Mary. *Making Noise, Making News: Suffrage Print Culture and U.S. Modernism*. New York, NY: Oxford University Press, 2017.

Chappell, Paul K. *Peaceful Revolution: How We Can Create the Future Needed for Humanity's Survival*. Westport, CT: Easton Studio Press, 2012.

Chenoweth, Erica and Maria J. Stephan. *Why Civil Resistance Works: The Strategic Logic of Nonviolent Conflict*. New York, NY: Columbia University Press, 2011.

Clift, Eleanor. *Founding Sisters and the Nineteenth Amendment*. Hoboken, NJ: John Wiley & Sons, 2003.

*Conkling, Winifred. *Votes for Women! American Suffragists and the Battle for the Ballot*. New York, NY: Algonquin Young Readers, 2018.

Cottrell, Robert C. *The Czech Republic: The Velvet Revolution*. Philadelphia, PA: Chelsea House, 2005.

Dalton, Dennis. *Mahatma Gandhi: Nonviolent Power in Action*. New York, NY: Columbia University Press, 1993.

Del Castilla, Richard G. and Richard A. Garcia. *Cesar Chavez: A Triumph of Spirit*. Norman, OK: University of Oklahoma Press, 1995.

Engler, Mark and Paul Engler. *This Is an Uprising: How Nonviolent Revolt Is Shaping the Twenty-First Century*. New York, NY: Bold Type Books, 2017.

Eskew, Glenn T. *But for Birmingham: The Local and National Movements in the Civil Rights Struggle*. Chapel Hill, NC: The University of North Carolina Press, 1997.

Ferriss, Susan and Ricardo Sandoval. *The Fight in the Fields: Cesar Chavez and the Farmworkers Movement*. New York, NY: Harcourt Brace & Company, 1997.

Gandhi, Mohandas K. *The Collected Works of Mahatma Gandhi*. New Delhi, India: Government of India, 1958.

———. *Satyagraha in South Africa*. Ahmedabad, India: Navajivan Publishing House, 1972.

Gandhi, Mohandas K. *Hind Swaraj*, New Delhi, India: Rajpal & Sons, 2011.

Ganz, Marshall. *Why David Sometimes Wins: Leadership, Organization, and Strategy in the California Farm Worker Movement*. New York, NY: Oxford University Press, 2009.

Gillmore, Inez Haynes Gillmore. *The Story of the Woman's Party*. London, UK: Forgotten Books, 2019.

Girard, Jolyon P., Darryl Mace, and Courtney Michelle Smith, eds. *American History through its Greatest Speeches: A Documentary History of the United States*. Santa Barbara, CA: ABC-CLIO, 2017.

Glenn, John K III. *Framing Democracy: Civil Society and Civic Movements in Eastern Europe*. Stanford, CA: Stanford University Press, 2001.

Guha, Ramachandra. *Gandhi Before India*. New York, NY: Alfred A. Knopf, 2014.

———. *Gandhi: The Years that Changed the World, 1914–1948*. New York, NY: Alfred A. Knopf, 2018.

Hampton, Henry and Steve Fayer with Sarah Flynn. *Voices of Freedom: An Oral History of the Civil rights movement from the 1950s through the 1980s*. New York, NY: Bantam, 1991.

Hardiman, David. *The Nonviolent Struggle for Indian Freedom, 1905–1919*. London, UK: Hurst Publishers, 2018.

Havel, Václav. *Open Letters: Selected Writings 1965–1990*. New York, NY: Alfred A. Knopf, 1991.

Keetley, Dawn and John Pettegrew, eds., *Public Women, Public Words: A Documentary History of American Feminism*. Lanham, MD: Rowman & Littlefield, 2002.

Kent, Susan K. *Sex and Suffrage in Britain 1860–1914*. London, UK: Routledge, 1990.

Ketels, Violet B. "'Havel to the Castle!' The Power of the Word." *The Annals of the Academy of Political and Social Science*. vol. 548, 45–69.

King, Martin Luther Jr. *Stride Toward Freedom: The Montgomery Story*. Boston, MA: Beacon Press, 2010.

*Kops, Deborah. *Alice Paul and the Fight for Women's Rights: From the Vote to the Equal Rights Amendment*. Honesdale, PA: Calkins Creek, 2017.

Krapfl, James. *Revolution with a Human Face: Politics, Culture, and Community in Czechoslovakia, 1989–1992*. Ithaca, NY: Cornell University Press, 2013.

Kukral, Michael A. *Theater of Revolution: A Study in Humantistic Political Geography*. Boulder, CO: Eastern European Monographs, 1997.

Kurlansky, Mark. *Nonviolence: The History of a Dangerous Idea.* New York, NY: Modern Library, 2008.

*Levinson, Cynthia. *We've Got a Job: the 1963 Birmingham Children's March.* Atlanta, GA: Peachtree Publishers, 2012.

Levy, Jacques E. *Cesar Chavez: Autobiography of La Causa.* Minneapolis, MN: University of Minnesota Press, 2007.

Long, Michael. *Making History: Czech Voices of Dissent and the Revolution of 1989.* Lanham, MD.: Rowman & Littlefield, 2005.

Lunardini, Christine. *Alice Paul: Equality for Women.* Boulder, CO: Westview Press, 2012.

Manis, Andrew M. *A Fire You Can't Put Out: The Civil Rights Life of Birmingham's Reverend Fred Shuttlesworth.* Tuscaloosa, AL: University of Alabama Press, 1999.

McWhorter, Diane. *Carry Me Home: Birmingham, Alabama: The Climactic Battle of the Civil Rights Revolution.* New York, NY: Simon & Schuster, 2001.

Moses, Greg. *Revolution of Conscience: Martin Luther King, Jr., and the Philosophy of Nonviolence.* New York, NY: Guilford Press, 1997.

Orosco, Jose-Antonio. *Cesar Chavez and the Common Sense of Nonviolence.* Albuquerque, NM: University of New Mexico Press, 2008.

Pawel, Miriam. *The Crusades of Cesar Chavez.* New York, NY: Bloomsbury Press, 2014.

Perry, Lewis. *Civil Disobedience: An American Tradition.* New Haven, CT: Yale University Press, 2013.

Rieder, Jonathan. *Gospel of Freedom: Martin Luther King, Jr.'s Letter from Birmingham Jail and the Struggle That Changed a Nation.* New York, NY: Bloomsbury Press, 2014.

Schell, Jonathan. *The Unconquerable World: Power, Nonviolence, and the Will of the People*. New York, NY: Metropolitan Books, 2003.

Schock, Kurt. *Unarmed Insurrections: People Power Movements in Nondemocracies*. Minneapolis, MN: University of Minnesota Press, 2005.

Sharma, Anand, ed. *Gandhian Way: Peace, Nonviolence, and Empowerment*. New Delhi, India: Academic Foundation, 2007.

Sharp, Gene. *The Politics of Nonviolent Action: Part One: Power and Struggle*. Boston, MA: Porter Sargent Publishers, 1973.

———. *The Politics of Nonviolent Action: Part Two: The Methods of Nonviolent Action*. Boston, MA: Porter Sargent Publishers, 1973.

———. *The Politics of Nonviolent Action: Part Three: The Dynamics of Nonviolent Action*. Boston, MA: Porter Sargent Publishers, 1973.

———. *Waging Nonviolent Struggle: 20th Century Practice and 21st Century Potential*. Boston, MA: Extending Horizons Books, 2005.

———. *Sharp's Dictionary of Power and Struggle: Language of Civil Resistance in Conflicts*. New York, NY: Oxford University Press, 2012.

Shaw, Randy. *Beyond the Fields: Cesar Chavez, the UFW, and the Struggle for Justice in the 21st Century*. Berkeley, CA: University of California Press, 2008.

Smithey, Lee A. and Lester R. Kurtz, eds. *The Paradox of Repression of Nonviolent Movements*. Syracuse, NY: Syracuse University Press, 2018.

Stevens, Doris. *Jailed for Freedom: American Women Win the Vote*. Troutdale, OR: NewSage Press, 1995.

Stiehm, Judith. *Nonviolent Power: Active and Passive Resistance in America*. Lexington, MA: Heath, 1972.

Stokes, Gale. *The Walls Came Tumbling Down: Collapse and Rebirth in Eastern Europe*. New York, NY: Oxford University Press, 2012.

Thompson, Gabriel. *America's Social Arsonist: Fred Ross and Grassroots Organizing in the Twentieth Century*. Berkeley, CA: University of California Press, 2016.

*Tougas, Shelley. *Birmingham 1963: How a Photograph Rallied Civil Rights Support*. Mankato, MN: Compass Point Books, 2011.

Vanek, Miroslav and Pavel Mucke. *Velvet Revolutions: An Oral History of Czech Society*. New York, NY: Oxford University Press, 2016.

Walton, Mary. *A Woman's Crusade: Alice Paul and the Battle for the Ballot*. New York, NY: St. Martin's Griffin, 2010.

Wheaton, Bernard and Zdenek Kavan. *Velvet Revolution: Czechoslovakia, 1988–1991*. Boulder, CO: Westview Press, 1992.

Younge, Gary. *The Speech: The Story Behind Dr. Martin Luther King Jr.'s Dream*. Chicago, IL: Haymarket Books, 2013.

Zahniser, J. D. and Amelia R. Fry. *Alice Paul: Claiming Power*. New York, NY: Oxford University Press, 2014.

Zantovsky, Michael. *Havel: A Life*. New York, NY: Grove Press, 2014.

Zumes, Stephen, Lester R. Kurtz, and Sarah Beth Asher, eds. *Nonviolent Social Movements: Geographical Perspectives*. Malden, MA: Blackwell, 1999.

IMAGE CREDITS

Pages i, v, 241, 248: Michael Campanella/Getty Images. **Pages ii–iii, 170–171:** Jon Lewis Photographs of the United Farm Workers Movement. Yale Collection of Western Americana, Beinecke Rare Book and Manuscript Library, Yale University. **Page vii:** TopFoto/The Image Works. **Page xii:** Marilyn Humphries/The Image Works. **Page 1:** Wallace Kirkland/Getty Images. **Page 9:** Roger-Viollet/The Image Works. **Page 20:** Copyright GandhiServe India. **Page 30:** Pictures from History/The Image Works. **Pages 32–33:** Dinodia Photos/Alamy Stock Photo. **Pages 37, 39, 46–47, 70, 79, 89, 188:** Library of Congress. **Pages 89, 188:** Bettmann/Getty Images. **Page 108:** AP Photo/*Atlanta Journal-Constitution*. **Pages 116–117, 126:** AP Photo/Bill Hudson. **Page 122:** Charles Moore/Getty Images. **Page 141:** AP Photo/File. **Page 143:** Take Stock/The Image Works. **Page 184:** Archives of Labor and Urban Affairs, Walter P. Reuther Library, Wayne State University. **Page 191:** Bob Fitch Photography Archive, Department of Special Collections, Stanford University Library, Stanford University. **Pages 192, 234**: CTK/Khol Pavel. **Page 193:** Joel Robine/Getty Images. **Page 198:** Jan Šibík. **Pages 200–201:** Josef Koudelka/Magnum Photos. **Page 234:** CTK Photo/Libor Hajsky (CTK via AP Images). **Page 239:** CTK Photo (CTK via AP Images). **Pages 256–257:** Tobias Schwarz/Getty Images. **Page 261:** Max Herman/NurPhoto via Getty Images.

ACKNOWLEDGMENTS

Thanks to:

Maya Savir, for spontaneously (and brilliantly!) suggesting nonviolence as the subject for my next book.

My agent, Dan Lazar, for working closely with me to turn that suggestion into a coherent book proposal. And for reliably advocating for me throughout the time since then.

My editor, Howard Reeves, for taking on this project and guiding its transformation from proposal to book.

Sara Sproull, for all manner of editorial assistance, especially in the tricky realm of photos.

The rest of the team at Abrams, for their diligent work in getting this manuscript into its best possible form.

James Krapfl, for sharing his thoughts about the Velvet Revolution.

The Peace Warriors of North Lawndale College Prep, for living this philosophy and providing inspiration to me and countless others.

My wife, Taal, for making it possible for me to do this work in the first place.

My dog, Bella, was (unbeknownst to her) my writing partner for over ten years. Together we wrote more than I ever could have alone. She will be missed.

INDEX

Note: Page numbers in *italics* refer to illustrations.

ABOUT THE AUTHOR

ARIEL HASAK-LOWY

Todd Hasak-Lowy is the author of several books for young readers. Hasak-Lowy is a professor in the department of liberal arts at the School of the Art Institute of Chicago and has a PhD from University of California, Berkeley. He lives in Evanston, Illinois, with his wife and two daughters.